First edition: 2005.

Self published

PHOTO CREDITS: Lisa Foster Carrillo pages:
 2 crab backs
32 fish head soup
36 corn chowder/okra soup
69 stuffed back breadfruit
87 hot & spicy shrimp
95 fish steaks
99 baked snapper
100 coconut fish
110 duck breasts with mango
113 curried chicken
117 curry glazed wings
129 suckling pig
138 stewed kidneys
155 flying fish & cou cou
170 rum pie, crème caramels & babas
227 pepperjellies & sauces
228 chutneys & chows

PHOTO CREDITS: John Marshall pages:
V L.A. Morley

COVER PAGE & SKETCHES: Gordon Parkinson

Other books by LaurelAnn Morley, *"Cooking with Caribbean Rum"*

Visit **www.lamorley.com** for ordering information on:
BOOKS and PRINTS (of these and other Gordon Parkinson's art sketches and original works)

ISBN 976-8082-07-0

To: Ms. Sarah Eddison, Memories of Caribbean life through food and art. Thank you for staying with my friends at Cobblers Cove, they are so special to me. LaurelAnn Dec 06

CARIBBEAN RECIPES
"Old & New"

Compiled	LaurelAnn Morley
Food prepared and styled	LaurelAnn Morley
Photography	LaurelAnn Morley and Lisa Carrillo - photot credits opposite page
Graphic Design/Layout	Samantha Bratt and Ideas from Designer Coast Inc. - Barbados
Cover Design	LaurelAnn Morley
Sketches	Gordon Parkinson (my Dad)
Publisher	Self published
Printed	Singapore

Herb tyre garden - both perfect as a way of recycling and making use of small spaces!

Contents

CHAPTERS

Pre ~ Chat

ACKNOWLEDGEMENTS

Through this book, I wish to acknowledge all the folks in the culinary industry, all those who have written recipes for us to enjoy, to our Caribbean street food vendors who through out the years have given me their invaluable information and inspiration to compile this book. To name one such vendor would be "Barry", who does belongs to Hart St. (his own words), Port of Spain, Trinidad selling peeled oranges at the side of the road, I promised to dedicate a book to him incorporating his cooking hints that he gave me. His recipe that I concocted for him is entitled 'Barry's Orange Fish".

DEDICATION

To my Mum: - Dickie Parkinson - Trestrail who taught me all I know and encouraged me in every walk of my life.

To my Dad - Gordon Parkinson for his wonderful sketches.

To my husband Trevor, my girls Judy and Laura who helped with the sampling.

To my brother Roger Parkinson for his patience and computer instructions. A field I am so dumb at!/Ha!

To Carol Bowen - she faithfully tested the recipes we used to photograph and went crab hunting for me.

To Gillie Coxall, and Margaret Murrey for all the background help in creating this book, from finding props to climbing coconut trees to assist me.

To Neil, my vegetable vendor for loaning me so many vegetables for both cooking and photographing.

To Mr. & Mrs. John Chandler at Fisherpond House for loaning me the use of their home and gardens.

To Pily - Lisa Carrillo for teaching me about food photography and for just being there for me.

To Graphic Photo Lab for their special care and encouragement with my photography.

To Jon Derr for so much email support.

To all my clients and friends who insisted I complete this book.

And finally and most importantly to all at DESIGNER COAST INC., Barbados - Simone, Loralie, and Kathy for invaluable graphic help - thank you girls!

Laurelann Morley

PREFACE

Laurel Ann Morley is a Caribbean person in all respects. A great believer in both preparing traditional Caribbean cuisine and promoting the use and substitutions of Caribbean produce to create new and exciting dishes.

She has worked as a caterer for the past 20 years, as a food consultant, as a food journalist for Caribbean Week newspaper and Barbados Holiday Guide, has written a cookbook entitled "COOKING WITH CARIBBEAN RUM" and has now opened a family run restaurant called THE COVE on the breathtaking, wind swept, East Coast of Barbados.

LAURELANN'S COMMENTS:

My idea of writing any cookbook is not only to share my recipes but to show in the photographs exactly what the finished product looks like, not some glossed up picture that when you try to reproduce the recipe it never looks like the dish you have just prepared. With this in mind, I have personally prepared all the food for photography myself, in most instances photographed it myself, to show a true form of the end product.

I believe strongly that food is part of our culture and heritage, one, which we as West Indians should never forget, never get wrapped up totally in International Cuisine and fast foods to the detriment of our tradition and legacy.

Where food is concerned it is amazing how many particular dishes we eat at specified times or festivals. What would Christmas be for a Trinidadian without their Pastelles (Spanish influenced), or for a Guyanese without their Garlic Pork (Portuguese influenced), or a Barbadian without their Jug Jug (Scottish-African adaptation) or for a Jamaican at Easter time without their Easter Buns. And certainly we would have to ask what Christmas for the entire Caribbean would be like without our home made drinks of Sorrel, Ginger Beer, Ponche Crema and Egg Noggs that we share in common with all the islands.

So to all who are born within our shores or visited our shores, we trust that you will enjoy these recipes, that you will teach your children and your children's children to prepare and delight in their ancestral cuisine.

ABOUT THE ARTIST MY DAD - GORDON PARKINSON

Born in Trinidad of Barbadian and Trinidad parentage.

SPORTS: A distinguished swimmer in his youth, holding numerous records in this field which remained unbroken for many a year.
His love for the sea and boats as reflected in many of his paintings stemmed from his love of sailing, a sport he not only excelled at, but encouraged so many people to pursue.

He left Trinidad for Venezuela where he and his brother started a company called "C.A. Parko", a water well drilling and supplies company. Around this time he married Dickie Trestrail from Trinidad and together the lot of us arrived. Rosemary, Myself, Brenda, Boydie and Roger.

Dad retired at aged 40 to live in Barbados and pursue his love of painting.
A self taught artist he allowed nothing to hamper his art. With no taught restrictions he experimented in every media available including shoe polish, with every tool available from paintbrushes, palette knives, sticks, papers and even vacuum cleaners to create various effects. Art became his world with exhibitions held in Barbados, Trinidad, Jamaica, Venezuela, U.S.A., Canada, England, and Belgium.

In the year 2001 he was honoured by Barbados for his extensive contribution to the arts by being chosen as the very first recipient of "The Nation Publishing Company Ltd.'s Lifetime Achievement Award for Art 2001".
He also received a personal plaque from 18 varying artistes "In appreciation of your inspiration and commitment to the arts and artistes over the years".

Here are some comments that appeared in Newspaper clipping about him and his art.
Artist, swimming champion in his hay day, yachtsman, engineer, weatherman, stargazer, philosopher,
female form watcher, whistler and magician.
Dad's quote "Everything that God has created has a basic beauty that is worth capturing."
"My painting has given me considerable enjoyment and I know that many owners of my work feel the same".
Newspaper comments. " Gordon Parkinson's exhibition is well rounded, colourful and presents a new facet of his talent for experimentation"
"Gordon Parkinson's work has always declared an almost forbidding facility of expression; as if he could paint anything he wanted to, in any style that he chose."

Alas, we lost the physical side of Dad on December 5th. 2004. But he lives on through memory, his wise sayings, his inventions and the amazing art that he was so prolific at. His legacy lives on through his art!
FOR VIEWING AND ORDERING GORDON'S PRINTS; Check out search engine: Gordon Parkinson as we will soon be launching a website or visit **www.lamorley.com**

Boats

Pre ~ Chat

An INTRODUCTION to CARIBBEAN CUISINE

The world is awakening to our wonderful Caribbean foods, like the Chinese, Italian, French world-renowned culinary meals; we are now becoming a force to reckon with and to stand equal to any of them.

Our foods are a potpourri of all the mixtures of races that abound in the islands. The original cooking of the Arawaks, Amerindians and Caribs, joined by a heavy African influence and added to by a touch of settlers such as English, Scottish in the smaller islands, Chinese and Indian in the larger islands with a pinch and a dash of Spanish, Portuguese, Lebanese and French influences have all combined to create a cuisine unique to us.

Our love for 'Seasoning', using freshly grown herbs and spices, ground or chopped fine to combine their flavours, added almost always with a bit of hot peppers for that added piquant flavour so cherished by us all throughout the Caribbean. Our methods of 'Browning' our stews and pelaos by both colouring and sealing in the natural goodness of the food.

Our wonderful array of 'Ground Provisions' as our starches such as yams, sweet potatoes, eddoes, tannias, breadfruit etc. are called.
Our extensive use of the magnificent exotic tropical fruits that abound and almost grow wild on our shores.
Our adding a dash or two of a bit of 'Rum' which almost all our islands take pride in producing what I consider to be the best rum in the world.
Our fresh and unusual vegetables. Our array of warm water fish and shellfish. All of these things team up to create our food heritage.

Fish Markets abound through out the islands and the local boisterous vendors will all have a tip and a hint as to how to prepare your fish. Nowadays with the advent of freezers, fish of all descriptions is available through out the year but I still find it best to visit the markets for the freshest catch of the day, as I tell my clients when they request fish as a meal, I like to look my fish in the eye and tickle their gills to ensure freshness. Like wise it is also best to visit local food markets for those vegetables and provisions picked just that morning.

Pork and chicken are extensively eaten and prized for their ability to combine with a variety of sauces, fruits and vegetables. I am a staunch believer that our pork is the finest in the world; perhaps it is because he is fed on our goodly provisions that make its flavour so special.

Each of our islands have their own unique recipes, particular and prized by them but in my research of the Caribbean cuisine as a whole, I have found many recipes that are basically similar with just a touch of some different ingredient according to the fancy of the islander. As an example, SALT FISH CAKES appear in every island, spices added vary in each recipe yet Trinidad has their version of ACCRA, which include yeast rather than baking powder as a leavening agent. Cassava breads appear in Jamaica, Trinidad, Guyana, and St. Vincent yet little known to Barbadians.

In Jamaica ACKEES are eaten yet nowhere else in the Caribbean are these consumed. In Trinidad PASTELLES are a Christmas season favorite and ROTIS were created there.

In Barbados we are the FLYING FISH capital with SEA EGGS (URCHINS) as a delicacy.

In the Bahamas, CONCH is prepared and eaten in a million ways yet although available through out the islands little in comparison is consumed by the rest of us.

Some form of COU COU appears through out the chain of islands but not really eaten in Jamaica.

Naturally with the advent of air travel, canning, freezers, and Caribbean people now moving from island to island, we have all combined these dishes to create a truly Caribbean feast.

What is so precious is our ability to name these recipes with such outlandish names as Jamaicans being very adept at this; such as "Stamp and go", "After burners", "Jerked Chicken", "Pinch me round", "Blue drawers", "Dip and Fall back", "Oil down" etc.

No special cooking utensils are needed in Caribbean cookery but for nostalgic reasons we should mention a few that are still to be found in most homes.

A "Swizzle Stick" usually a stick with a metal rounded infusion of wire or a plain stick with smaller branches used for stirring up drink concoctions or soups.

A "Coneree"- A special clay pot with a cover for cooking up those delicious 'Pepperpots' and Stews.

A "Coal Pot" in both metal and clay forms, used for outdoor cooking by many vendors.

A "Plateen" or "Tawa" used for making Roti Flaps and flat breads.

A "Black Pan" or "Buck Pot"-a heavy iron pot or pan used for any and everything, carefully seasoned and passed on from generation to generation.

A "Cou Cou Stick"- A Barbadian cooking utensil in the form of a flattened cricket bat used in making all the various Cou Cous.

A "Mortar and Pestle"- Marble or wooden used in grinding herbs and spices, and among other things pounding plantain to make Foo Foo and pounding salt fish for Frizzled Salt Fish.

A "Kreng Kreng"- Basket used to smoke and preserve meats.

A "Calabash"- used for serving meals or transporting water.

A "Pot Spoon"- long handled large stirring spoon used for everything imaginable.

A "Matapee"- Long woven tool used to squeeze and extract liquid from Cassava.

Pre ~ Chat

Caribbean fruits

AN A-Z of CARIBBEAN FOODS

Ackee - A tree vegetable – the fruit ripens to a bright red colour then opens to expose the edible part a pale golden flesh. Ackees are poisonous if not allowed to fully ripen and open on their own. Iit is advisable to get an experts' advise on when to reap.

Accra - Salt fish fritter made with yeast.

Akkra - Originally a black-eyed pea fritter of African origin.

Allspice - The berries resemble black peppercorns with a combined flavour of spices such as nutmeg, cinnamon and clove. Also known as pimiento and Jamaica Pepper.

Annatto - Rusty red seed used to make colouring for foods by soaking in warm oil.

Arrowroot - Starch mostly grown in St. Vincent used for thickening gravies, sauces and in desserts.

Aubergine - A purplish vegetable resembling mushrooms in flavour. Known as eggplant, melongene or garden egg.

Avocado - Pear shaped used mostly in salads. Also known as simply "Pear", "Midshipman's Pear", "Zaboca" and "Alligator Pear".

Baby Squash - Small delicate flavoured squash, best served with a dab of butter and one herb.

Bajan - Refers to anything or anyone of or from BARBADOS.

Bananas - Both green and ripe bananas are eaten in the Caribbean, the green are prepared in many ways and eaten as a vegetable. Boil in their skins or peeled then added to the meal.

Pre ~ Chat

Banana Leaves - Used to wrap foods in prior to cooking

Black Pudding - A sausage made of starches and spices traditionally served with Souse on a Saturday. Each island has its own variation of fillers such as rice in Guyana, bread in Trinidad, sweet potato in Barbados and cassava in the smaller islands.

Breadfruit - Brought to the islands by Captain Bligh from the Pacific Islands in the 1790s.
Breadfruit is mostly served as a starch and is so versatile that at last count I have thought of a least 30 ways of preparing it. For most recipes, peel, core slice into 8 sections and boil in salted water before proceeding with a recipe.

Breadnut - A cousin to the Breadfruit, the tree and fruit are fairly similar but the actual seeds are eaten. Resembles Chestnuts in both look and flavour.

Callaloo - Both the root and leaves are eaten. The root is served as a starch while the leaves are made into tasty vegetable and soup dishes. The leaves are eaten as a vegetable or in many soups and are known as Dasheen.

Cassareep - Extract from Cassava prepared and used as a natural preservative and to impart a unique flavour in Guyanese Pepperpot.

Cassava - Also known as Yuca or Manioc. A starch popular from Arawak times. Ground and dried as in Farina, boiled or fried, used in meal preparations, breads and desserts such as Cassava Pone.

Chocho - A vegetable widely known as Christophene or Chayote.

Coconut - What a tree! From the trunk we get Coconut Heart of Palm, an old dried trunk is used as a chopping block or to tie our orchids on, the mesh found at the base is used to line plant baskets with. From the leaves we weave various mats, hats and decorations. From the fruit in its green form we chill and drink the 'Coconut Water' probably one of the most refreshing Caribbean drinks then go on to savour the soft jelly lining the coconut. When dried, the husk is used in potting soil, the flesh is grated and used to make coconut milk, cream and oil. Literally there is no part of the entire tree that is not used. Even for leisure, what a sweet feeling to sling a hammock between two coconut trees and just simply relax in tropical splendour.

Conch - A large mollusc also known as "Conk", "Lambie". The meat tends to be rather tough so should be tenderised by pounding it. Eaten raw in salads or cooked in soups, stews and fritters. The shell is used for decorative purposes and as a horn in many islands.

Conkies - Cornmeal usually mixed with pumpkin, raisins, coconut, spices with or without meat then wrapped in banana leaves and steamed.

Coo Coo - Another spelling version. See Cou Cou.

Coriander also known as cilantro or Chinese parsley.

Pre ~ Chat

Cou Cou - African term used to refer to mashing of starches and vegetables to form a rather firm pudding like dish. Corn cou cou is the most famous but so delicious are the green banana cou cou and the breadfruit cou cou. So popular in Barbados they have developed a special stick for stirring the cou cou.

Crapaud - Also known as "Mountain Chicken" it is a special breed of frog famous in Dominica.

Creole - Totally local to any island.

Dasheen - Leaves or the bulb of the taro used in soups and as a vegetable. Spinach is a fair substitute.

Eddoes - Tuber belonging to the yam, tannia and taro family. Usually cooked whole in their skins then peeled and prepared in dishes or peeled chopped and added to soups and stews.

Farine - A flour make from grated and sun dried cassava.

Festival - A dumpling based on cornmeal.

Fish Tea - A fish broth made with fish heads and bones, vegetables etc. and highly spiced.

Ginger root - Gnarled brown root used extensively in Caribbean cooking for in both savoury and sweet dishes. Keep wrapped in plastic in the refrigerator it will last several weeks.

Ground Provision - THAT WHICH THE GROUND PROVIDES - Term used to describe tannias, sweet potatoes, eddoes, yams etc.

Guava - Oval to rounded shaped fruit, eaten raw or cooked into a sweet dessert stew. Guavas are also used in making jams, jellies and Caribbean confection.

Guinea Corn - An African type of sorghum used in making Barbados's Christmas Jug Jug.

Gungo peas - Also known as Pigeon peas

Heart of Palm - Tender hearts or shoots taken from core of the top of the palm trees. My favourite is the coconut heart of palm, used in making salads.

Hot peppers - An integral part of Caribbean cooking, the most famous are the Scotch Bonnets, the Wiri Wiri and the Bird Peppers and lets not forget the Bajan Bonnie pepper so difficult to come by.

Jamaican pepper - See Allspice

Jerk - A seasoning and term used in the preparation of Jamaican barbecues.

Jug Jug - A Christmas specialty in Barbados consisting of stewed and ground pigeon peas mixed with meats, herbs and guinea corn, said to be a substitute by the Scottish settlers for their Haggis.

Pre ~ Chat

Mace - See Nutmeg.

Mamey Apple - A relative of the mango family with thick brown outer skin and orangish flesh inside.

Manish Water - A thick spicy soup made of Goat offal with vegetables and starches added.

Mauby - Also spelt as Mawby. A drink made from the bark of a tree combined with spices to produce a bitter sweet flavour. Excellent thirst quencher.

Mountain chicken - See chapraud

Nutmeg - Grown extensively in Grenada. Used grated in food preparation as well as in baking and topping of our exotic drinks. The outer red part on the shell of the fruit is the Mace.

Occroes/Okra - Brought from Africa, this green pod like vegetable is one of those one either hates or loves, there is no happy inbetween for these. Integral part of Caribbean cuisine and prepared in so many different ways.

Otaheite Apple - Known as Pomerac.

Papaya - See paw paw.

Pawpaw - Tropical fruit used when ripe in desserts, when green in preparation of hot sauces, pickles, as a cooked vegetable and in candies. The leaves act as a natural tenderiser for meats.

Pigeon Peas - Very popular in Caribbean cooking and served almost daily in the form as peas and rice. Also used in soups and stews.

Pimiento - See Allspice.

Plantain - Cousin to a banana but always cooked and served as a vegetable. The sweet flavour of a very ripe plantain helps counteract the spicy food of the Caribbean.

Pomerac - Red skinned pear shaped fruit eaten raw or used for desserts or jams.

Roti - Flat bread of Indian origin served as a bread with curry meals or used to wrap curried meats and vegetables forming a type of sandwich so loved by all West Indians.

Rum - Both golden and white are produced through out the islands and are considered the best in the world. An alcoholic spirit used in drinks, desserts and added to many dishes to enhance their flavour.

Sea Eggs or Sea Urchins - The white variety is a delicacy in Barbados, eaten both raw and cooked.

Shaddock - Thick skinned large citrus fruit used for making sweets - the original fruit from which the grapefruit was developed.

Sorrel - A must for Christmas. Sorrel is prepared as a drink, a liqueur, in jellies.

Soursop - Large green heart shaped fruit with slight tangy flavour, used in drinks, desserts and ice cream.

Souse - A combination of boiled pork, preferably tongue, feet, ears and flap, seasoned and marinated in cucumber, onion, hot pepper, parsley and limejuice. Usually offered with Black Pudding.

Sweet Potato - A tuber served as a starch and prepared in numerous ways.

Tamarind - Pod from a tree. Remove outer hard shell, place in bowl with a little hot water to extract juice. Use in drinks, chutneys, sweets and curries.

Tannia - Relative to the eddoe, yam family, peeled and used as a starch on its own or in soups and stews.

Taro - The bulb of the dasheen, see dasheen.

Yams - Come in various varieties used as a starch.

Known as "Ground Provisions: 1. Yam   2. Sweet Potatoes   3. Tannias   4. Cassava   5. Eddoes

Light Houses of Barbados

"Coconut tree shadows" by Gordon Parkinson

Starters & Snack Foods

Fisherpond Plantation Great House, BARBADOS. Formal dinning setting by kind permission of Mr. & Mrs. John Chandler who open their premises for private functions.

In days of old, starters were served mainly in the Old Plantation homes as part of a great sit down formal meal. Today, with the informality of Caribbean get togethers, it is usually passed around with drinks before a meal. For this reason I have included FRITTERS in this section for they make excellent crispy morsels to nibble on before that anticipated spread of food to come.

I am delighted to see more and more Caribbean foods used at cocktail parties. Today's Caribbean cocktail functions are designed to include as many tasty tidbits as you can muster and make you feel in the end as if you have had an entire meal. Use your imagination in converting other recipes to smaller bite sized versions for passing. And remember to serve heavier two-to-three bite morsels towards the end to 'sop up and sober up'. Good examples of these would be Mini Rotis, small Jamaican Beef Patties, medium sized hot bread rolls stuffed with ham or fried fish to resemble mini Bajan cutters.

Examples:

: Serve thick Trinidadian Callaloo soup as a dip with FOO FOO (plantain Balls) on a toothpick for dipping into the soup.

: Similarly try preparing a thick sauced Barbadian Salt Fish Stew as a dip and make tiny Corn COU COU balls to dip in.

: Perhaps a miniature portion of Fish and Bakes.

: Try cutting fish into fingers, seasoning and preparing according to the island and served with a cocktail or avocado sauce as a dip.

: Cut Pudding and Souse into bite sizes and insert toothpicks.

: Make small kebabs out of jerked chicken, pork or fish. These are best barbecued outdoors where the scent of the sizzling kebabs tantalizes you with anticipation of what is to come.

Starters & Snack Foods

Crab backs - delicious as a starter or as a light meal with a little buttered toast

Ingredients for preparing Solomon Gundy

CRAB BACKS *(the most popular item on our menu at The Cove. Mixture may be placed in scallop shells and baked as directed)*

Meat from 12 fresh crabs or 1 lb. crabmeat
4 Tbsps. butter
¼ cup minced onion
1 tsp. fresh thyme
2 Tbsps. chopped fresh parsley
4 chives chopped
2 garlic cloves minced
Small hot pepper minced
1 tsp. Worcestershire sauce
Juice from ½ lime
Salt and pepper to taste
½ cup breadcrumbs plus ¼ cup water.

Scrub 8 of the crab backs. Melt butter in medium saucepan, fry onion till soft, add thyme, parsley, chives, garlic, hot pepper, Worcestershire and fry for a few minutes more, add crab meat, limejuice, salt, pepper, crumbs and water. Mix well. Fill shells. Bake in a preheated 375F. Oven for 20 minutes. SERVES 8.

CRAB & CHEESE *(Delicate and different)*

1 lb. cooked crabmeat
2 Tbsps. sherry
¼ cup fresh breadcrumbs
¼ tsp. chopped hot pepper
Juice from ½ a lime
6 Tbsps. cream
¼ cup chopped fresh chives
Dash of Worcestershire sauce
Salt and pepper to taste
Freshly grated cheese for topping

Combine all ingredients except cheese in a bowl, mix well. Divide equally amongst 6 buttered crab shells or scallop shells. Top with grated cheese and bake in a preheated 375F. Oven for 10-15 minutes. SERVES 6.

One of those dishes whose naming baffles many.

SOLOMON GUNDY

3-4 smoked herrings
1 onion chopped
½ hot pepper minced
2 tsps. vinegar
2 Tbsps. olive oil
1 Tbsp. Rum
Chopped parsley to garnish

Soak herrings in water to cover till 4-5 hours or till soft. Remove skin and bones. Mash with remaining ingredients except tomato and parsley to make a paste. Serve on toast garnished with tomato wedges and sprinkled with parsley.

SOLOMON GUNDY BUTTER: Mix 1-2 tsps. Solomon Gundy mixture from above with 2-3 Tbsps. softened butter. Spread on crackers.

PATTIES *(patties are served through out the islands at cocktail parties and as a midmorning snack. They vary slightly between islands with Jamaica having its own distinct spices)*

Prepared pastry - puff or short crust.

2 lbs. minced beef (ground)
4 Tbsps. butter
2 large onions chopped
1 garlic clove minced
1 Tbsp. each chopped fresh parsley, thyme
½ tsp. fresh marjoram
Small piece hot pepper minced
6 blades chive chopped
1 Tbsp. Worcestershire sauce

Heat butter, fry onions and garlic 2-3 minutes, add beef, parsley, thyme, marjoram, hot pepper and fry till browned. Add 1 cup water or stock, Worcestershire and cook adding more liquid if needed for 30 minutes. Salt and pepper to taste. Cool mixture completely.

Roll pastry out on a floured surface and cut into 6" circles or 4" for cocktail size, brush one edge with beaten egg, place 1-3 Tbsps. filling (depending on size cut) in centre, fold over, seal and place on greased baking sheet. Brush with additional egg and bake in a preheated 400F. Oven for 20-25 minutes. MAKES about 20 patties.

PATTIES - JAMAICAN *(the most famous of all!)*

FILLING
4 Tbsps. butter
2 onions chopped fine
4 chives chopped fine
2 tsps. fresh thyme minced
2 garlic cloves minced
½ hot pepper minced
1 ½ lbs. minced beef (ground)
1 Tbsp. curry powder
1 tsp. cumin seed
Dash of ground allspice
4 tomatoes chopped
¼ cup water
Salt and pepper to taste
¼ cup breadcrumbs
2 egg yolks beaten with 1 Tbsp. water

PASTRY
1 lb. flour
2 tsps. turmeric powder
1 tsp. salt
½ lb. butter or diced suet
6-8 Tbsps. iced water

FOR PASTRY: Combine flour, turmeric and salt. Cut in butter to resemble large breadcrumbs, add water and combine to form a pastry. Chill 30 minutes.

FOR FILLING: Heat butter, fry onions, chives, thyme, garlic, hot pepper 3-4 minutes, add beef, curry powder, cumin, and allspice. Cook till browned 5 minutes, add tomatoes, water, salt and pepper to taste. Cook till most of the liquid is absorbed. Add breadcrumbs and cool. Roll out pastry and cut into 6" circles, brush sides with egg mixture and place about 2 Tbsps. meat mixture in centre. Fold in half and crimp edges with a fork to seal, place on greased baking sheet. Coat tops with egg, prick tops with a fork and bake in a preheated 400F. Oven for 25-30 minutes. MAKES approximately 30 patties.

Patties may be prepared in advance and frozen. To reheat: place on a cookie sheet in a single row, preheat oven to 400F. Bake 10 minutes if defrosted and 15 minutes if frozen.

Jamaican beef patties - served as a midmorning snack through out the islands: made in miniature form are excellent hors d' oeuvres

Flying fish rows & melts with toast points

Bul jol

Avocados are grown in almost every Caribbean backyard.

AVOCADO AND SHRIMP SALAD

1 large avocado cut in ½"cubes
24 medium sized poached cold shrimp
Thousand Island dressing- preferable Caribbean style - *see index for recipe*
1 lime cut in four wedges
Salt and pepper to taste
4 large lettuce leaves, shredded
4 bacon slices cooked crisp and crumbled
Place lettuce on each of four dishes, place avocado in center and carefully place 6 shrimp around the avocado. Drizzle with Thousand Island dressing or serve separately and top with the crumbled bacon. Serve with lime wedge and salt and pepper. SERVES 4.

FLYING FISH ROWS & MELTS

1 pkg. flying fish rows and melts
1 tsp. limejuice
Salt and pepper to taste
1 Tbsp. each butter and oil
1 onion sliced thin
1 garlic clove minced
2 blades of chive chopped
1 tsp. fresh thyme chopped
Small piece of hot pepper minced
Rinse rows and melts, pat dry. Season with limejuice, salt and pepper. Let rest 10 minutes. Heat butter and oil in a frying pan. Add onion and garlic, cook till soft. Add chive, thyme and hot pepper. Cook stirring 2-3 minutes. Add rows and melts and fry till browned 3-5 minutes. Serve over toast points. SERVES 4.

FRIED FLYING FISH ROWS & MELTS

Season rows and melts with salt, pepper, limejuice and either " Bajan or Jerk" seasoning - *see recipe in index.* Dip in flour, then beaten egg diluted with a little milk and finally in dry breadcrumbs. Fry till golden.

Also known as Salt Fish Souse. My Mum often served this for Sunday breakfast at home as prepared and refrigerated overnight it is an instant breakfast for late risers.

BUL JOL *(Also spelt as BOWL JOWL, BRULE JOLL and Others)*

½ lb. salt fish, soaked overnight in water to cover- cooked or uncooked
2 onions chopped small
4 blades chive chopped
2 tomatoes chopped small
½ green sweet pepper chopped small
¼ cup olive oil
2-4 Tbsps. fresh limejuice
Small piece hot pepper minced
Cut fish into small cubes or flake. Place in a bowl with remaining ingredients using limejuice to taste. Adjust flavouring with more oil or limejuice if necessary. Diced avocado may be added. Excellent hors d 'oeuvres served with crackers at a party, or serve with bakes - *see index*. SERVES12.

OYSTER COCKTAIL *(Sold at roundabouts and street corners in Trinidad when oysters are in season. Try substituting smoked oysters for cocktail parties in saved and scrubbed oyster shells)*

48 fresh oysters
1 tsp. hot pepper sauce
2 Tbsps. grated onion
1 cup tomato ketchup
1 tsp. Worcestershire sauce
Salt to taste
Juice from 1 lime or more to taste
1 tsp. chopped chadon bene or cilantro (optional)

Combine hot pepper sauce with onion, ketchup, Worcestershire, salt, limejuice and chadon bene. Either place dollops of sauce on opened oyster shells to serve or marinate oysters in sauce before serving. Serve well chilled.
SERVES 4-8.

AUBERGINE or EGGPLANT SPREAD

1 large aubergine (eggplant) unpeeled
2 Tbsps. grated onion
½ clove garlic minced
1 tsp. sugar
2 Tbsps. limejuice
2 Tbsps. olive oil
1 Tbsp. chopped parsley
Salt and pepper to taste

Steam eggplant 15 minutes or till soft. Drain and pat dry, remove flesh from skin. Mash flesh with remaining ingredients adding salt and pepper to taste. Chill. Serve with crackers. MAKES 1 cup.

CURRY CHUTNEY DIP *(My favourite, especially made with homemade chutney)*

1x8 oz. package cream cheese
1 tsp. curry powder
3-4 Tbsps. chutney

Place all ingredients in a blender to mix. Add additional curry or chutney to taste. Serve with crackers; cold boiled deveined shrimp or green fruit slices such as mango or golden apple. MAKES 1 cup of dip.

FLYING FISH PATE

6 flying fish
Dried ground ginger
Salt and pepper to taste
1 small onion finely chopped
Small piece of hot pepper finely minced
3 ozs cream cheese softened and creamed
2 chives chopped
1 Tbsp. chopped fresh parsley
Limejuice to taste

Season flying fish individually with salt, pepper and a little ground ginger. Steam in about 4 Tbsps. of water for 2 minutes per side. Remove from pan and cool. Flake by hand into small pieces and combine with remaining ingredients, adding more limejuice, salt, pepper and hot pepper to taste. CHILL. Best served with "Wibix"or "Crix" crackers.

Starters & Snack Foods

Oyster cocktail, fiery and delicious

Starters & Snack Foods

Top Channa, bottom Pholouri Balls - I grew up snacking on these

Left - Plantain chips, Middle- Coconut chips and Right - Breadfruit chips

My Auntie Joan used to bring these home for us after the horse races in Trinidad. Wrapped in brown paper cone shapes. They are now available prepared in bottles.

CHANNA *(Also known as chick peas or garbanzo peas)*

1 pkg. small split dried channa
1 hot pepper minced
Salt

Soak channa in water overnight; rub channa in a kitchen towel to remove skins, parboil channa till very firm but cooked. Drain, dry on kitchen paper. Heat oil for deep fat frying, add hot pepper to oil and fry channas till golden, remove from oil, drain and salt to taste.

PHOLOURI BALLS *(Serve these with home made chutney as a dip)*

1 lb.split pea flour
5 garlic cloves minced
½ tsp. each ground cumin and fresh thyme
2 tsps. curry powder
2 seasoning peppers finely chopped
½ hot pepper minced
2 tsps. baking powder
1 tsp. salt plus lots of freshly ground coarse black pepper
1 cup water

Combine all the dry and herb ingredients. Beat in the water slowly. Allow to rest for 30 minutes. Fry by tablespoonfuls in hot oil till golden. Serve with fresh mango chutney - *see index for recipe.*

PLANTAIN CHIPS

4-5 green but full plantains
Oil for deep fat frying
Salt

Peel plantains, cut in wafer thin slices, fry in oil till lightly browned and crisp. Sprinkle with salt and serve.

COCONUT CHIPS

1 dry coconut
Salt to taste

Crack coconut, remove from shell and peel off brown skin. Using potato peeler, slice off thin slices of coconut and place on a greased cookie sheet. Bake in a preheated 400F. Oven for 10 minutes, watching carefully and turning often. Salt to taste. Serve warm or cool and store in an airtight container.

Parboiled breadfruit, sliced thin can also be used, omit the soaking in salted water.

BREADFRUIT CHIPS

1 breadfruit, cored peeled and cut into very thin slices.
Lots of salted water
Oil for deep fat frying
Salt to taste

Soak breadfruit slices in salted water for 30 minutes or more. Drain and dry thoroughly on paper towels. Deep fat fry till crisp and golden. Sprinkle with additional salt and serve.

Starters & Snack Foods

Several of theses make a meal unto themselves. For entertaining serve Baras in a bread basket, with the Channa perhaps in a chaffing dish and bowls of Kucheela, Chutney and Hot sauce.

DOUBLES

1 lb.dried channa soaked overnight in water to cover (chick peas/garbanzo peas)

4 Tbsps. oil

2 onions chopped

3 Tbsps. curry powder

1 Tbsp. whole cumin seed

5 garlic cloves minced

1 hot pepper minced

Salt and pepper to taste

Accompaniments of: Hot pepper sauce/Homemade mango Kucheela and Chutney/Bara breads - *see index for recipe*

Heat oil, fry onions till golden. Add curry powder, cumin seed, garlic and hot pepper. Fry 2-3 minutes. Add soaked channa and water to cover. Cook till peas are tender and most of the liquid evaporates. Add salt and pepper to taste. MAKES filling for 15-20 Doubles.

YEAST BARAS *(Substitute Split Pea Baras for a faster Bara version - see recipe in index)*

2 cups flour

1 tsp. turmeric

½ tsp. salt

½ tsp. baking powder

1 tsp. ground cumin

¾ cup warm water

2 tsps. active dry yeast

Pinch of sugar

Sift flour, turmeric, salt, baking powder and cumin into a large bowl. In another bowl mix warm water with yeast and sugar, allow to rest for 5 minutes. Combine yeast and flour mixtures kneading well to form a soft dough. Let rest two hours, covered in a large greased bowl. Divide dough into 10-12 pieces and shape into balls, then flatten or roll out into 4-5 inch rounds. Set aside for 10 minutes. Heat oil in a frying pan, fry Bara 1-2 minutes per side. Drain on paper toweling. MAKES 10-12.

Although available in most West Indian supermarkets, try making this home version.

KUCHEELA

2 cups coarsely grated green mango flesh

3 garlic cloves minced

1 hot pepper minced

2 tsps. curry powder

About ½ cup mustard oil

Place grated mango in a cheesecloth and wring out as much liquid as possible. Spread mango on a cookie sheet and place in the sun to dry for a few hours. Combine dried mango shreds with remaining ingredients, mixing well and adding enough mustard oil to make a thick soupy consistency. Place in jars and put in the sun turning often for several days.

TO ASSEMBLE: Place some of the Channa mixture on one Bara bread, add pepper sauce and Kucheela to taste. Top with another Bara bread to make a sandwich or place Channa on one Bara, add condiments, fold in half or DOUBLE OVER!

Starters & Snack Foods

Doubles - a combination of curried Channa, Kucheela, Chutney, Hot sauce and Bara bread

Starters & Snack Foods

Shrimp with Sweet and Sour dip

Top - Chicken wings with Orange Glaze, Bottom - with Hot Hot Glaze

Starters & Snack Foods

SHRIMP & DIPS

Peel, devein and boil medium sized shrimp in salted water 2-3 minutes. Drain immediately; bring to room temperature and chill. Insert toothpicks in each shrimp and serve with one or two of the following dipping sauces.

CURRY/CHUTNEY MAYO DIP: Combine ½ cup mayonnaise with:
1 tsp. curry powder
2 Tbsps. mango chutney

HERBED DIP: Combine ½ cup mayonnaise with:
2 Tbsps. each chopped chives and parsley.
Juice from ½ a lime

SWEET & SOUR DIP: In a saucepan combine ½ cup tomato catsup with:
Juice from 1 lime
¼ cup or more to taste Caribbean brown sugar
Pinch of powdered cinnamon
Heat till sugar is dissolved

GLAZED CHICKEN WINGS

These little morsels are very popular at parties. You will need to prepare masses of them.

EITHER: Salt and pepper chicken wings, place on a baking tray. Brush with melted butter and bake in a preheated 425F. Oven for 20 minutes.
Glaze with one of the following glazes and continue baking for a further 15-20 minutes or till cooked through.

OR: Place wings on a preheated oiled barbecue or coal pot and cook as above.
Place on a platter and serve additional Glaze as a sauce for dipping. Can be served hot or at room temperature.

PEPPERJELLY GLAZE: Melt Pepper Jelly - *(see recipe in index)* in microwave, brush on wings.

HOT HOT GLAZE: Combine 1 cup ketchup, 2 Tbsps. hot pepper sauce, ¼ cup Caribbean brown sugar with juice from 1 lime, brush on wings.

GUAVA JAM GLAZE: Melt ½ cup guava jam in microwave with ¼ cup butter, brush on wings.

ORANGE GLAZE: Combine ½ cup orange marmalade with 1 Tbsp. each prepared mustard and honey.

PINEAPPLE GLAZE: Combine ½ cup pineapple jam with a 4 oz. tin crushed pineapple well drained and ¼ cup Caribbean brown sugar in a small saucepan. Cook till jam and sugar are dissolved then add 1 tsp. soy sauce.

These little crispy morsels are served at weddings, tea parties and children's parties.

CHEESE STRAWS

½ lb. butter
½ lb. sharp cheddar cheese grated
Dash of pepper sauce
½ lb. flour
Pinch of salt and pepper
Cream the butter, cheese and pepper sauce, add flour, salt and pepper to make dough. Place in icing bag and pipe out in ribbons 2" long on a greased baking sheet. Bake in a preheated 350F.Oven for 7-10 minutes. Store in airtight jars. MAKES about 1½ lbs. cheese straws.

CHEDDAR PUFFS

½ cup grated cheddar cheese
½ cup fresh breadcrumbs
2 eggs well beaten
2 Tbsps. butter softened
⅓ cup milk
½ tsp. Caribbean pepper sauce
1 tsp. baking powder
Dash of salt and black pepper
Mix all ingredients thoroughly, Place in well greased miniature muffin pans and bake in a preheated 400F Oven for 15-18 minutes or till golden. Let rest in pans 15 minutes, remove and serve warm or at room temperature. MAKES around 24 puffs.

CHEESE ROLLS

12 slices sandwich bread
Cheddar cheese cut into fingers about ¼" thick
Mustard and pepper sauce to taste.
Melted butter
Remove crusts from bread, flatten with a rolling pin and spread with thin layer of mustard and pepper sauce mixture. Place a cheese finger on the bread slices and roll up tightly jelly roll fashion, set on a tray seam sides down and close together to hold. Repeat till all rolls are prepared. Refrigerate or freeze till firm. Cut rolls in half. Brush with melted butter, place on buttered baking sheet and bake in preheated 450F. Oven for 5-6 minutes till golden. Serve warm. MAKES 12 TOASTS.

CHEEDAR CROCK

1½ cups grated sharp cheddar cheese
1x3oz. package of cream cheese
¼ cup each of butter and cream
½ tsp. dry mustard powder
Dash of Worcestershire sauce and hot pepper sauce
2 blades of chive chopped
1 Tbsp. minced parsley
Blend all ingredients except chives and parsley in a food processor. Fold in chives and parsley. Place in a crock dish or dip dish and refrigerate overnight to blend flavours. Take out 15 minutes before using and serve with crackers. SERVES 16.

A combination of cheese hors d' oeuvres: Puffs, Rolls and Cheese Crock

Salt Fish cakes, so popular through out the Caribbean at cocktail parties

Salt Fish cakes exist in every Caribbean island with each having its own particular version according to seasonings added. In Grenada they are called SALT FISH CUTTERS, in Jamaica STAMP AND GO, in Barbados sometimes known as AFTER BURNERS.

SALT FISH FRITTERS OR CAKES

8 ozs. salt fish, soaked in water overnight (raw or cooked, your preference)
2 onions chopped finely
4 blades chive chopped
½ a hot pepper minced
2 tsps. fresh thyme
1 cup flour
1 heaping tsp.of baking powder
1 tsp. "Jamaican Jerk or Bajan Seasoning" optional - *see recipe in index*
¾ cup water
Salt and black pepper to taste
Oil for deep fat frying
Remove skin and bones from salt fish, chop fine with the onion, chive, hot pepper and thyme. Add flour, baking powder, "seasoning", water and salt and pepper to taste. Fry by teaspoons in hot oil. Serve on toothpicks with hot dipping sauce.

For a variation try ACCRA - Trinidad origin, using yeast as the rising agent and served with FLOATS or a FRIED FLOUR BAKE - (See recipe in index)
To the above recipe substitute the flour, baking powder with:
2 cups flour, 2 tsps. dried yeast, 1½ cups warm water.
Place yeast in warm water to soften for 10 minutes, add to salt fish mixture and beat in the flour. Allow to rest for 2 hours. Fry and serve as above recipe.

DIPPING SAUCE *(for Salt fish fritters)*
Combine 1 cup ketchup with 2 Tbsps. hot sauce and 1 Tbsp. Worcestershire sauce.

I often substitute curried split peas for the potato in this recipe. Also try using chopped dasheen leaves or curried pumpkin.

ALLOO PIE *(Indian origin from Trinidad & Tobago)*
4 cups flour
1 tsp. salt
2 Tbsps baking powder
3 Tbsps. butter
2 Tbsps. butter-additional
1 large onion chopped
1 Tbsp. curry powder
½ tsp. cumin seed
1 garlic clove minced
4 large potatoes, cooked and coarsely mashed
1 Tbsp. chadon benne or coriander leaves minced
Combine flour, salt and baking powder. Cut in 3 Tbsps. of the butter. Add a little warm water to make a soft dough. Set aside for 30 minutes. Heat remaining 2 Tbsps. butter and lightly fry the onion, curry, cumin and garlic till soft. Add the mashed potato, chadon bene and mix till combined. Cool. Roll the dough out on a lightly floured surface, cut in 6"or 3" rounds, place filling in center and fold to make a crescent shape, sealing edges completely. Deep fat fry.
MAKES about 30.

All of these fritters may be served as a vegetable with any main meal.

PUMPKIN FRITTERS

1 lb. steamed, peeled pumpkin
1 egg beaten
8 Tbsps. or more of flour
1 tsp. of baking powder
Pinch of salt
1 tsp. sugar
Dash of cinnamon
Oil for frying
Drain pumpkin thoroughly. Mash pumpkin with all ingredients except oil. Fry in hot oil by tablespoonfuls. Drain on paper towels and serve. *Optional: May be sprinkled with sugar and cinnamon before serving.* MAKES about 30 cocktail sized fritters.

PLANTAIN FRITTERS

Substitute equal amount of mashed over-ripe plantain for Pumpkin in above recipe.

TANNIA FRITTERS *(When Mum prepared these as part of the meal, they were mostly consumed prior to arriving at the table)*

3-4 tannias, peeled and very finely grated (2 cups grated)
3 blades chive chopped
½ tsp. salt
¼ tsp. freshly ground black pepper
Small piece hot pepper minced
1 heaping tsp. baking powder
2-3 Tbsps. flour
Oil for frying
Mix all ingredients except oil. Rest for 10 minutes. Heat oil in a frying pan, fry by teaspoonfuls till golden. Drain on paper towels and serve. MAKES around 30 fritters.

A specialty at my restaurant, even children who do not like spinach eat these in large volumes. A good way to introduce them to the flavour of spinach.

SPINACH FRITTERS

½ lb. fresh raw spinach, chopped fine
2 chives chopped
Dash of Worcestershire sauce
½ cup milk
½ cup flour
1 heaping tsp.of baking powder
1 egg beaten
½ cup fresh breadcrumbs
½ onion chopped
Salt and pepper to taste
Freshly grated nutmeg
Oil for frying
Combine all ingredients except oil. Rest for 10 minutes. Fry in hot oil by tablespoonfuls. Drain and serve. MAKES about 30 cocktail sized fritters.

Two views of Sandy Island in the Grenadines

Chattel houses of Barbados

Soups & One Pot Meals

Chattel house with laundry hanging out to dry, a typical soup day!

I have grouped Soups and One-Pot Meals together for both are often prepared for household meals where nothing else is served, they are extremely hearty and nutritious containing one or several meats, starches, vegetables and herbs, plus the added feature of requiring little supervision time in their preparation.

Strangely enough, we hardly ever prepare cold soups which one would more imagine in this our Tropical climate but hearty and piping hot is what we clamour for because to us it is THE MEAL in itself.

BREADFRUIT features a lot in these type meals for almost every other home has a tree growing in their backyard. Breadfruit is sometimes available tinned but do not down cry me! Although not a substitute try combining sweet potato and English potato for the breadfruit, at least the gorgeous cookups of the Caribbean can be prepared with a vague semblance to the original.
CALLALOO may be substituted with spinach.
SALT FISH as we speak of it is available in most countries in Italian/ Portuguese/Latin American specialty shops as "Bacalao".

Both types of meals stemmed from busy days when the housewife had little time to prepare a three or four part meal. Market days and laundry days are two such days for these meals.

In Jamaica they are known as Saturday Soups (Market day) yet in other Caribbean islands as Monday Soups (Laundry day).

Soups are also often served at the end of a party in many islands to help absorb the amount of liquor consumed and to sober up the individual.

Soups & One Pot Meals

The ultimate soup - Callaloo Soup with crab

Pumpkin soup

Traditionally land crabs known as blue crabs or swampies are used in the preparation of this soup but sea crabs may be used. Omit crab and use small shrimp instead or substitute chicken chunks or diced boneless fish if you are not a seafood person.

CALLALOO SOUP WITH CRAB *(Trinidad)*

1 ham bone
¼ lb. salt pork, soaked overnight in water to cover
2 cups water
4 Tbsps. butter
2 onions chopped
½ tsp. minced fresh hot pepper
1 clove garlic minced
4-5 sprigs of fresh thyme
½ lb. okras, sliced thin
1 lb. callaloo leaves, chopped
4 cups chicken stock
2 crabs, feet and claws
½ lb. fresh or tinned crab meat
1 cup of coconut milk
Salt and pepper to taste

Cook salt pork and ham bone in the 2 cups of water for 2 hours or till pork is tender, cut up pork into small pieces and remove any ham from bone, reserve meat and stock. Meanwhile heat butter in large saucepan, fry onions, hot pepper, garlic and thyme for 2-3 minutes, add okras and fry 2-3 minutes longer, add reserved liquid and meats from salt pork, callaloo leaves and chicken stock. Bring to a boil, reduce heat and simmer for 30 minutes or till soft and cooked. Swizzle or puree in blender, return soup to pan, add crab, coconut milk and continue cooking 10 minutes or till crab is cooked. Season with salt and pepper to taste. SERVES 6.

Often served with Foo Foo, - see index. If made very thick with lots of additional meat, serve it over a bowl of fluffy white rice to make an entire meal out of this dish.

Can be garnished with a thin cream and topped with freshly grated nutmeg or cinnamon
PUMPKIN SOUP

3 Tbsps. butter
1 large onion grated
Small clove garlic minced
1 tsp. fresh thyme
Small piece hot red pepper minced
1 sweet potato grated
2 carrots grated
6 cups good home made chicken stock
6 cups grated pumpkin
Salt and pepper to taste

Heat butter in a saucepan, add onion and cook 2-3 minutes, add remaining ingredients and cook till potato, carrots and pumpkin are reduced to a chunky puree. Salt and pepper to taste. Sprinkle with just a touch of nutmeg or cinnamon if liked before serving. SERVES 6.

Wonderful also cooked a little longer until thickened more and served over rice as a meal.

PEANUT SOUP

1 chicken cut into joints

Salt and pepper to taste

1 Tbsps. paprika

4 Tbsps. corn oil

3 large onions minced

5 Tbsps. peanut butter

3 Tbsps. tomato paste

5 fresh tomatoes chopped

3 bay leaves

1 Tbsp. fresh minced basil

¼ tsp. freshly grated nutmeg

2 chicken stock cubes

8 cups water

Season chicken with a little salt, pepper and the paprika. Lightly brown the joints in the corn oil. Remove from pan and set aside. In the same pan fry onions 3-4 minutes, add peanut butter, tomato paste, fresh tomatoes, bay leaves, basil and nutmeg. Fry 3-4 minutes. Return chicken to the pan, add stock cubes and water, bring to a boil, reduce heat and simmer 1 hour or until chicken is cooked. Adjust flavour with salt and pepper to taste. SERVES 6.

Devised as a means of using up bits and pieces of provisions grown on the plantations. In Dominica a SANCOCHE SOUP is made with salt fish, the provisions are omitted and the soup served with a sprinkling of fresh limejuice.

BEEF SANCOCHE

4 Tbsps. oil

4 large onions chopped

2 garlic cloves minced

¼ lb. salted pigtail cut into small pieces, soaked overnight in water to cover

½ lb. salt beef cut into small pieces, soaked overnight in water to cover

2 lbs. stew beef

1 Tbsp. fresh thyme

10 cups beef stock or 4 beef cubes dissolved in 10 cups water

½ lb. dried split peas washed

½ lb. each cassava, eddoes, yam cut into 1"cubes

1 lb. each sweet potato and English potato cut into 1"cubes

1 hot pepper minced

1 cup coconut cream

3 green plantains or 6 green bananas peeled

Salt and pepper to taste

Dumplings if desired - *see recipe in index*

Heat oil in a large saucepan, fry onions 3-4 minutes till soft, add garlic, meats and thyme and fry stirring 3-4 minutes. Add stock and split peas, simmer gently for 1 hour. Add cassava, eddoes, yam, potatoes, hot pepper and coconut cream; cook 20 minutes or till provisions are tender. Add plantain or green bananas and dumplings if desired, continue cooking 10-12 minutes longer. Salt and pepper to taste. SERVES 6.

Peanut soup with a difference

Soup tureen of Split Pea Soup, ready to serve

Split pea soup is a tradition in our family, in fact my Mum serves it every Christmas Eve at her open house parties, and guest jokingly tell her they come for her pea soup alone.
I prepare it when my children go on their late night parties such as Old Years Night to eat as they come home and it is a must on my Sunday buffet at The Cove.
In olden days a soup was traditionally served at the end of a party to help absorb the liquor consumed, a tradition I have tried to revive in my catering deals always using a split pea soup.
The chicken after cooking may be omitted from the soup and used for a follow up dish, chicken salad or cookup.
Sweet Nutmeg dumplings go beautifully with this soup - see recipe.

SPLIT PEA SOUP

1 ham bone or piece of salt beef or pigtail
1 chicken, cut into serving pieces
1 package of yellow split peas
4 sprigs fresh thyme
8 cups water or chicken stock
2 garlic clove minced
2 onions chopped fine
Piece of hot pepper minced
1 carrot cut into small cubes
1 small sweet potato cut into small cubes
Small piece of pumpkin, peeled and cut into small cubes
Salt and pepper to taste

Rinse split peas in a colander till liquid runs clear. Place ham bone or salted meat in a large saucepan, bring to a boil, lower heat and simmer till meats are tender, about 1½ hours; or pressure cook 20-30 minutes. Remove meat and cut away from bones, set aside. To the stock add the chicken, cook 20-30 minutes or till chicken is cooked, remove chicken and set aside. Add peas, thyme, garlic, onion, and hot pepper, cook until peas are almost a puree about 1 hour. Add carrots, sweet potato and pumpkin. Return all meats to the soup and salt and pepper to taste. Cook 30 minutes more. SERVES 6.

QUICK VEGETABLE SOUP

2 Tbsps. butter
1 large onion chopped
2 garlic cloves minced
2 vegetable stock cubes dissolved in 4 cups water
1 cup of coarsely chopped mixed vegetables such as: Carrots, christophenes, butternut squash, pumpkin, string beans, cauliflower, cabbage etc.
2 cups of peeled diced yam, eddoes, sweet potatoes or a combination of any or all
1 tsp. fresh chopped thyme
Piece of hot pepper minced

Heat butter in a saucepan, fry onion and garlic till soft, add remaining ingredients and cook till vegetables are soft and tender. Adjust flavour with salt and pepper to taste. Dumplings may be added-see index.
The beauty of this soup is the many variations of vegetables that can be substituted, just use any and all of your personal favourite. You can also omit the starches for a lighter version.
SERVES 2.

In Antigua a similar dish is served, the shrimp, ground provisions and coconut milk are omitted and substituted with chunks of pumpkin, green papaw and fresh green peas, using less water to obtain a more stew like consistency.

PEPPERPOT JAMAICAN SOUP

¼ lb. salt beef, cut into ½" pieces, soaked overnight in water to cover

½ lb. salt pork, cut into ½" slices, soaked overnight in water to cover

1 lb. stew beef

2 onions chopped

8 cups water

1½ lbs. callaloo - dasheen leaves chopped

½ lb. kale leaves chopped

12 okras (occroes) sliced thin

½ lb. each yam, coco (taro, dasheen root) peeled and diced

1 each green pepper, hot pepper diced

1 clove garlic minced

4 chives, chopped

4 tsps. fresh thyme

¾ cup coconut milk

¼ lb. shrimp

1 Tbsp. butter

Salt and pepper to taste

Place salted pork, salted beef and stew beef in a saucepan with the onions and the water, bring to a boil, lower heat and simmer for 2 hours or alternatively place in pressure cooker and cook 30 minutes. Add the callaloo and kale and continue cooking for 15-20 minutes. Set aside the meats and puree the soup, return to the saucepan. Add okras, yam, coco, sweet pepper, hot pepper and garlic. Cook 30-40 minutes. Add chives, thyme and coconut milk. Cook 15 minutes more. Add shrimp and butter, cook 5 minutes more. *(Dumplings may be added with the chives etc.)* SERVES 10.

Corn soup is sold on many a street in Trinidad and is also popular at parties served at the end of a long drinking and partying night. SERVES 10.

CORN SOUP

5 fresh ears of corn

8 cups chicken stock

¼ lb. salt beef or pig tail cut into small pieces, soaked overnight

1 chicken cut in pieces

1 large onion chopped fine

2 tsps. fresh thyme,

Piece of hot pepper minced

1 cup milk

Salt and pepper to taste

Grate the corn directly into a large saucepan ensuring that as much milk as possible is extracted. Add all other ingredients except salt and pepper and bring to a boil, lower heat and simmer for 2 hours stirring often. Salt and pepper to taste. *(The chicken may be deboned and served with the soup or reserved for serving as part of a meal.)* SERVES 6.

Corn soup made with fresh corn

Soups & One Pot Meals

A bowl of Eddo Soup

Fish head soup, so prized by Caribbean folk

Soups & One Pot Meals

EDDO SOUP

1 lb. eddoes, peeled and cut into small pieces
2 cups chicken stock or 1 chicken stock cube dissolved in 2 cups water
2 Tbsps. butter
2 onions minced
3 blades chive chopped
Small piece hot pepper minced
Salt and pepper to taste
1 cup milk

Melt butter in a saucepan, fry onions, chives, hot pepper and eddoes for a few minutes over low heat, add stock, bring to a boil and cook covered till eddoes are soft. Mash eddoes against side of pan leaving some lumps, add salt and pepper to taste then the milk. Rewarm and serve. SERVES 4.

For BREADFRUIT SOUP or TANNIA SOUP, substitute equivalent amounts of the particular 'provision' for the eddoes and add pigtail or salted beef stock and a bit of coconut cream near the end of cooking time.
Optional: Serve garnished with bread, lightly buttered, sprinkled with parsley and grilled till top is delicately golden.

Dozens of distinctive fish soups, chowders and 'broths' are prepared in the Caribbean, with each island particularly known for their special version. In Jamaica they are famous for their "FISH TEA", in Trinidad you have to go to the fish market by the ferry port for their fish soup my sister calls "HANGOVER SOUP", in the Bahamas it is their "CONCH CHOWDERS" and in Barbados their "DOLPHIN HEAD SOUP" prized by most fisher folk. This soup is my version of a combination of the islands cooking. Chunks of shredded cabbage, okras and chopped callaloo leaves may also be added and naturally, some dumplings always make a more genuine West Indian Soup.

CARIBBEAN FISH SOUP

Bones and head from 1-2 dolphins (dorado), soaked in juice from 1 lime for 10 minutes
Piece of salted pigtail, soaked in water overnight and cut into small pieces
3 Tbsps. butter
2 large onions minced
6 chopped chives
½ cup each chopped celery and carrots
1 tomato chopped
2 cloves of garlic minced
4 fresh sprigs of thyme minced
½ hot pepper minced
2 cups diced tannias, eddoes, yam, sweet potato, green bananas. Any one item or a combination of as many as are available.)
1½ lbs. any or preferably a combination of chunks of boneless fish meat.
Lots of chopped parsley for garnish

Boil fish bones, head and pigtail in 6 cups water for 1 hour. Strain, reserving fish stock and pig tail meat. Carefully remove all fish from bones, reserve the fish. Heat butter, fry onions, chives, celery, carrots, tomato, garlic, thyme for 5 minutes. Add reserved fish stock, pigtail and hot pepper. Bring to a boil, lower heat and simmer 30-40 minutes or till pigtail is soft. Add tannias, eddoes etc. cook 20 minutes more, add the chunks of boneless fish and the reserved fish from the stock. Simmer 10 minutes. Season with salt and pepper if needed and garnish with parsley. SERVES 6.

In many Caribbean recipe books, conch is not only pounded to tenderize but also cooked for an hour or more before using. I find this elongated cooking time totally unnecessary and treated like any shellfish (a few minutes of cooking) retains the tenderness. Like all shellfish. DO NOT OVERCOOK!

BAHAMAS CONCH CHOWDER # 1

5 cleaned and pounded conch

3 Tbsps. butter

2 leeks, sliced thin

1 large onion chopped

4 potatoes peeled and diced

3 blades of chive chopped

Small piece of hot pepper minced

2 cups chicken stock

½ cup white wine plus an additional 2 Tbsps.

1 cup cream

Salt and pepper to taste

Diced red sweet pepper to garnish

Cut or shred conch into small pieces, set aside. Melt butter in saucepan, add leeks, onion and fry till soft but not browned about 4 minutes. Add potatoes, chives, hot pepper, stock, ½ cup of wine and boil till potatoes are cooked, about 20 minutes. Stir in conch, add cream, additional wine and salt and pepper to taste. Simmer 2-4 minutes or till heated through. Garnish with diced red sweet pepper. SERVES 4.

CONCH CHOWDER SOUP # 2

3 lbs. conch ground

Salt and pepper to taste

3 Tbsps. limejuice

3 Tbsps butter

¼ lb. bacon diced

3 large onions chopped

1 lb. can tomatoes coarsely chopped, liquid reserved

1tsp. fresh thyme

2 bay leaves

2 sprigs parsley chopped plus additional for garnish

Small piece hot pepper minced

3 cups water or fish stock

¼ cup sherry

1 Tbsp. Worcestershire sauce

4 potatoes, peeled and diced small

Combine conch, limejuice, salt and pepper to taste mixing well, set aside. In large pan heat butter and bacon, cook till bacon fat is rendered, add onions and cook till soft but not browned. Add tin of tomatoes with liquid, thyme, bay leaves, parsley, hot pepper and water or stock. Bring to a boil, lower heat and simmer 40-45 minutes. Add sherry, Worcestershire and potatoes, return to the heat, bring to a boil and cook over medium heat 20 minutes or till potatoes are cooked. Add prepared conch, season with additional salt and pepper to taste. Cook for 3-4 minutes longer. Garnish with parsley. SERVES 6.

Soups & One Pot Meals

Bahamas Conch Chowder #1

Caribbean Corn chowder - my girls love this one

Okra Soup

Soups & One Pot Meals

CARIBBEAN CORN CHOWDER *(I cook this for my girls regularly)*

2 Tbsps. butter
4 slices of bacon, cut into ½" pieces
1 onion chopped
4 slices ham cut into ½" cubes
Small piece hot pepper minced
1 tsp. fresh chopped thyme
4 cups peeled diced potatoes
1x16 oz. tin of whole kernel corn with liquid
1x8 oz. tin creamed corn
4 cups milk

Heat butter and bacon in a large saucepan, fry onion 3-4 minutes. Add ham, hot pepper, thyme, potatoes, both corns and milk. Bring to a boil, lower heat to medium and cook 20 minutes or until potatoes are tender. Salt and pepper to taste. SERVES 4.

This soup is very popular through out the islands, not only is it hearty and delicious but extremely nourishing as well.

COW HEEL SOUP

4 lbs. cow heel cut in 3" pieces
1 tsp. salt
4 chives, chopped
3 large onions chopped
4 carrots sliced
6 garlic cloves minced
1 Tbsp. fresh sprigs thyme chopped
1 hot pepper left whole
¼ tsp. black pepper
Ground provisions such as one or a variety of: yams, cassava, sweet potato, eddoes etc.

Boil heel with water to cover in a pressure cooker for 1 hour or on the stove for 3 hours till very soft and tender. Remove heel, cut the meat from the bones and return the meat to the pot, add remaining ingredients and cook for 30 minutes until the provisions are cooked and tender. SERVES 6.

You have got to love Okras as I do for this soup, made very thick it is gorgeous served over plain boiled rice.

OKRA SOUP

3 Tbsps. butter
1 onion grated
3 cups sliced okras
1 garlic clove minced
Small piece hot pepper minced
½ tsp. fresh thyme
4 cups chicken stock or 1 chicken cube dissolved in 4 cups water
2-3 eddoes peeled and cut into ½" dice
½ cup chopped: one or combination of: chicken/ salt fish/ ham/ crab meat/ shrimp/conch.

Heat butter in saucepan, add onion and cook 2-3 minutes, add okra and cook 3-4 minutes, add garlic, hot pepper, thyme and stock. Cook 15-20 minutes. Whisk or swizzle soup to get a creamy consistency, add eddoes and cook 10-12 minutes more. Add chopped meat and continue cooking for 5 minutes. SERVES 4.

Soups & One Pot Meals

BOIL-UP

Chunks of fish, any one kind or a variety of fish
Pieces of peeled breadfruit, green bananas and eddoes
Seasonings of chive, green pepper, hot pepper, thyme and onion
Salt and pepper to taste
3 Tbsps. butter or olive oil
fresh lime juice

Place breadfruit, green bananas and eddoes in a pot, sprinkle seasonings on top, place fish chunks over this, salt and pepper to taste, barely cover with boiling water, bring to a boil, reduce heat and simmer 30 minutes or till vegetables are tender and most of the liquid has evaporated. Dot with butter or olive oil and sprinkle with limejuice just before serving.
SERVES: according to volume of ingredients.

Fabulous way to use up left over fish. Any fried fish will do.
BAJAN FISH PIE

4 bacon rashers, cut in 1" slices
1 large onion sliced
1 Tbsp. flour
1 cup milk
Dash of Worcestershire sauce
Dash of hot sauce
Salt and pepper to taste
6 cooked fried flying fish or any boneless fried fish, cut in quarters
2 large tomatoes sliced
1 lb. yam mashed with a little milk, butter, salt and pepper (potato may be substituted)
Buttered crumbs for topping or grated cheddar cheese

Heat the bacon in a pan till fat is rendered, add onion and cook 3-4 minutes, add flour and cook 1 minute. Add milk in a slow steady stream and cook stirring till thickened. Add Worcestershire and a dash of hot sauce if desired. Salt and pepper to taste. Place half the fish in a casserole, top with half the sauce, 1 of the tomatoes. Repeat layers. Top pie with yam, cover with crumbs or cheese and bake in a preheated 375.F. Oven for 25 minutes. SERVES 4-6.

SALT FISH PIE *(Mum often prepared this for the family)*

1 lb. salt fish soaked overnight, deboned and cut into chunks and parboiled
4 chives chopped
Small piece hot pepper
1 tsp. of fresh thyme
2 lbs. English potatoes or yam, peeled, boiled and sliced thin
1 large onion thinly sliced
1 tomato sliced thin
2 cups milk, mixed with 2 Tbsps. flour
2 hard boiled eggs, sliced
Paprika for garnish

Combine fish with the chive, hot pepper and thyme. Layer greased casserole dish with half each of the salt fish mixture, sliced onion, tomato, egg and potatoes. Repeat layering. Pour milk over, top with dabs of butter. Bake in a 375F oven for 30 minutes. SERVES 4-6.

Mum's Salt Fish Pie

Soups & One Pot Meals

Hot Zaboca (Avocado) and Farine

Okra & Callaloo Rice Up

This dish is served quite often in Grenada, Trinidad and Tobago and a similar version appears in the French speaking Caribbean islands. The avocado is often mashed but I being an avocadoholic like the look of the slices and to mash my own on my plate.
Make sure you have lots of gravy to soak up the farine.

HOT ZABOCA (AVOCADO) AND FARINE

8 ozs. salt fish soaked overnight, deboned and shredded

4 Tbsps. olive oil

2 onions coarsely chopped

2 tomatoes, coarsely chopped

2 garlic cloves minced

1 tsp. fresh thyme chopped

½ hot pepper finely chopped

1 cup water

Salt and pepper to taste

Cassava meal or farine

1 avocado peeled, coarsely crushed or thinly sliced

Parsley to garnish

Heat oil in saucepan. Fry onions 3-4 minutes till golden, add tomatoes, garlic, thyme, hot pepper and water. Bring to a boil, reduce heat and simmer till tomatoes are mushy and a good sauce consistency is made, about 20 minutes. Add salt fish and cook 2-3 minutes. Adjust seasoning with salt and pepper to taste if necessary. To serve, place a serving of salt fish on a plate, sprinkle with cassava meal and lay slices of or mashed avocado over top. Garnish with parsley if desired. SERVES 6.

TO MAKE FARINE: Finely grate some cassava, place it on a tray and let sit in the sun till dried. Place dried cassava in a food processor and grind till fine crumbs are formed.

Use either shrimp, fish, a combination of the former two or chunks of boneless chicken. I cook this often as a one-pot meal.

OKRA & CALLALOO RICE-UP

1 lb. of any of the above mentioned meats

Salt and pepper

4 Tbsps. butter

1 each garlic clove minced, large onion coarsely chopped

Small piece hot pepper minced

2 tsps. fresh thyme minced

12 okras sliced into 1" slices

1 lb. callaloo washed and sliced into 1" slices or substitute spinach

2 cups chicken stock or 1 stock cube dissolved in 2 cups water

1 cup rice

½ cup coconut milk

Salt and pepper meat being used. Heat butter in a saucepan, fry meat till cooked, remove and set aside. Fry garlic, onion, hot pepper, thyme and okras 3-4 minutes. Add callaloo, fry 2 minutes, add stock and rice. Return meat to pan, bring to a boil, reduce heat, cover and simmer till rice is cooked.

Add coconut milk, cover tightly and leave covered, off the heat for 10 minutes. SERVES 4.

Wonderful accompanied by fried plantain, perhaps some bakes and a good tossed salad.

Soups & One Pot Meals

This is a great example of Chinese influence in Caribbean foods. This dish is my daughter's favourite, I chop everything up and cook the noodles in advance and then she takes over the final cooking. Beef, shrimp or pork may be substituted and you may add as many other fresh vegetables as you would like.

CHICKEN CARIBBEAN CHOW MEIN

1 Tbsp. oil- for frying the chicken
1 pkg. chicken tenders, rinsed, patted dry and cut into long strips
2 cloves garlic minced
Salt and pepper to taste
Additional 3 Tbsps. oil – for frying the chow mein
1 large onion sliced thin
4 chives chopped
1" piece of fresh ginger grated
1 sprig of fresh thyme minced
Small piece hot pepper minced
1 stalk of celery sliced
3 carrots cut into thin strips
2 cups cooked string beans
¼ of a cabbage sliced thin
1 red sweet pepper sliced thin
8 ozs. cooked egg noodles, drained
2 Tbsps. soy sauce
1 tsp. cornstarch dissolved in 4 Tbsps. water
1 chicken stock cube.

Lightly salt and pepper the chicken, coat with the minced garlic till well combined. Heat 1 Tbsp. oil in a large saucepan, stir-fry chicken till golden and cooked, remove and set aside. Heat additional oil in the same saucepan, add onion, chives, ginger, thyme, hot pepper, celery, carrots, string beans, cabbage and sweet pepper; stir-fry till vegetables are tender but still crisp. Return chicken with any accumulated juices to pan with vegetables and cook 2-3 minutes more. Combine soy sauce, cornstarch, water and chicken cube, add to saucepan along with the noodles and stir-fry till noodles are coated and heated through. Add additional soy sauce, salt and pepper to taste. SERVES 6.

Very delicately flavoured dish, a wonderful one pot meal, serve with store bought shrimp wontons to add a crunch to the meal.

NOODLE AND SHRIMP POT

8 ozs. of noodles
½ lb. shrimp, cleaned and deveined
1 tsp. MSG (Optional)
3 eggs
4 blades of chive chopped
Small piece hot pepper minced
1" piece of fresh ginger minced
Salt and black pepper to taste
Additional chopped chives for garnish
Dash of soy sauce

Soak noodles in water for 5 minutes, cut into 6" lengths. In a medium sized saucepan put the noodles to boil with 1 cup of water or chicken stock. When the noodles are cooked and most of the water evaporated, add the shrimp, MSG, eggs, chives, hot pepper and ginger stirring constantly. Salt and pepper to taste. Garnish with chives. Sprinkle with soy sauce. SERVES 2

Caribbean Chicken Chow Mein

Soups & One Pot Meals

Chicken Cook-up, use this recipe as a guideline, adding to suit your taste

Every island has a special cook-up, the beauty of this recipe is that it is to be used as a guide-line only for in all cook-ups it is a matter of using what you have on hand, omitting some ingredients and adding others to suit.

CHICKEN COOK-UP

2 salted pig tails, cut up and soaked overnight

1 chicken cut into serving pieces

4 whole cloves

4 garlic cloves minced

3 large onions chopped coarsely

Pieces of peeled tannia, eddoes, yam, dasheen root

4 green bananas peeled and halved

2 celery stalks chopped

1 Tbsp. each fresh parsley and thyme chopped

½ a hot pepper minced

1 lb. peeled cubed pumpkin

Cornmeal dumplings if required - *see recipe in index*

Limejuice to serve

Chopped parsley for garnish (optional)

Cook pigtail in 5 cups water till soft, about 1-1½ hours, add remaining ingredients except pumpkin, dumplings and limejuice. Bring to a boil, reduce heat and cook till chicken and ground provisions are almost tender about 20 minutes. Add pumpkin, cook 15 minutes longer. If serving cornmeal dumplings add with the pumpkin, cover and allow the dumplings to steam. Serve sprinkled with limejuice. Garnish with parsley. SERVES 6.

Breadfruit Metagee is of Guyanese origin, real soul food! Like most Caribbean foods, spellings vary. Sometimes called Mettem, sometimes spelt Mettegee. I've seen it prepared where limejuice is sprinkled over the top with lots of fresh chopped chives sprinkled over the entire meal just before serving.

BREADFRUIT METAGEE

1 lb. mixed salt beef and salted pigtail, soaked overnight

1 lb. salt fish, soaked overnight and deboned

1 breadfruit, cored, peeled and sliced

1 lb. yam or sweet potatoes or a mixture of both, peeled and cut in large chunks

6 large onions chopped

2 whole hot peppers

Bunch of fresh thyme tied together.

2 cups coconut milk - *see recipe in index*

½ lb. peeled diced pumpkin

12 okras

EITHER: 2 firm but ripe plantains, peeled and cut in quarters

OR: 5 green bananas peeled and cut into quarters.

Boil salted meats (not fish) till tender, about 1 hour. Drain and reserve some liquid to add to the dish. In large saucepan place breadfruit, yam or sweet potatoes or both, salted meats, onions, hot peppers and thyme. Pour coconut milk over the entire mixture, add some of the reserved broth. Cover pot and cook slowly until starches are cooked about 25 minutes. Place pumpkin, plantains, or bananas, okras and salt fish on top. Cover again and simmer about 15 minutes more or until cooked through, adding more meat stock if required. Remove hot peppers and thyme before serving. SERVES 6-8.

One of those dishes that can be prepared in advance and heated up just before serving.
Try substituting plantain slices for the aubergine.
Try omitting aubergine altogether to create a Caribbean shepherd's pie

AUBERGINE/EGGPLANT BEEF PIE

1 large aubergine (eggplant), peeled, thinly sliced
3 Tbsps. oil
3 onions chopped fine
1 garlic clove minced
1½ lbs. minced (Ground) beef
4 tomatoes chopped fine
2 Tbsps. chopped fresh parsley
1 tsp. each chopped fresh marjoram and thyme
¼ piece of hot pepper minced
¼ tsp. fresh grated nutmeg
Dash of powdered clove
Salt and pepper to taste
Cooked yam/or breadfruit/or English potato mashed with a little milk, butter and salt
Grated cheddar cheese for topping

Heat oil in a large frying pan, fry aubergine in batches till just soft and golden, place in a layer in bottom of casserole dish. Fry onions and garlic in same pan till onions are just soft, add beef and cook stirring till browned, add tomatoes, parsley, marjoram, thyme, hot pepper, nutmeg, clove and salt and pepper to taste. Cook till tomatoes are soft and meat cooked through. Place mixture over aubergine in casserole. Top dish with mashed yam or breadfruit or potato, cover with grated cheese and bake in a preheated 375F Oven for 30 minutes.
SERVES 4.

From Tobago, you need time to sit and pick the crab.
Try substituting shrimp in their shell or chunks of Lobster tail or Crayfish.
Try substituting pieces of jointed chicken - allow to cook longer.
This dish is absolutely gorgeous in its simplicity of ingredients and flavour.

CURRIED CRAB AND DUMPLINGS

4 large crabs, cleaned and backs removed
3 Tbsps. butter
2 Tbsps. curry powder
1 large onion chopped
1 tsp. fresh thyme chopped
2 garlic cloves minced
2 tsps. fresh ginger grated
1 cup coconut milk
Salt and pepper to taste

DUMPLINGS - *see recipe in index*

Heat butter in large saucepan, fry curry powder, onion, thyme, garlic and ginger 3-4 minutes. Add coconut milk and crabs, cover and bring to the boil, add dumplings, lower heat and simmer for 20 minutes. Salt and pepper to taste.
SERVES 2.

Serve this with some roti flaps or buss-up shots - see index, to dip into the gravy. Or over a bowl of hot steaming rice.

Aubergine Beef pie

Curried Crab & Dumplings

Pudding & Souce - A Saturday special through out the islands

PUDDING AND SOUCE: *Traditionally served on Saturdays. SERVES 10.*
OLD WIVES TALES: To make Pudding is an art onto itself. My first attempt ended up with one enormous mess in the pot as the skins burst producing an inedible mush. One advice given to me was to simmer it gently and no noise must be made or the pudding would burst. I smiled for I could see no reason for noise disturbing the contents of a pot! But duly, my second attempt ensured that my family whisper and then only outside the kitchen. Lo and behold, I forgot I had dogs as they barked away my skins burst again! My third attempt after much research was to line off the pot with either brown paper or banana leaves to ensure the skins do not touch the metal of the pot BUT trust you me… I took no chances … my children, husband and dogs were sent out in the neighbourhood, phone off the hook and voila glorious pudding!

TO PREPARE CASINGS: Turn the pig casings inside out and run them through the water faucet to clean. Rub them with salt and limejuice and soak for 1 hour. Rinse, turning inside out again and repeat rinsing through the faucet. *(Place an open end of the casing over the kitchen faucet, hold tightly and run the water through.)*

TO STUFF CASINGS: Use a sausage stuffer according to manufacturer's directions or place casing over the narrow end of a large funnel, tie with soft string and slowly add the pudding mixture using the rounded side of a wooden spoon to stuff the mixture in. Tie at regular intervals using soft string.

BARBADOS PUDDING

2-3 lbs. sweet potatoes, peeled and grated	½ tsp. black pepper
6 chives chopped	3 Tbsps. sugar
2 tsps. each fresh thyme and marjoram	**EITHER:** ½ cup fresh pig's blood (optional)
¼ tsp. powdered cloves	**OR:** ¼ cup 'browning''- *see recipe in index*
2 tsps. salt	1½ cups pork stock or water
1 hot pepper minced	3-4 feet approximately of pig casing

Prepare casings as above. Line a large pot with brown paper or banana leaves. Meanwhile combine the sweet potato, chives, thyme, marjoram, cloves, salt, hot pepper, black pepper and sugar in a food processor or blender in batches and process till pureed. Add pig's blood or browning if used and some of the pork stock from the Souce or water, puree to a smooth consistency. Stuff casings as above. Place pudding in lined pot, add cold water to cover, bring to a boil, reduce heat immediately and barely simmer for 40-45 minutes. After about 20 minutes, prick slightly with a needle. Pudding may also be steamed without the pig casing over a double boiler.
In GUYANA - Recipe substitutes cooked rice for the sweet potato.
In TRINIDAD - Recipe substitutes bread for the sweet potato.
In OTHER ISLANDS - Recipe substitutes farine or cassava for the sweet potato.

SOUCE *(Some islands, make souse from cooked CONCH or TRIPE)*
MEATS: Half a pig's head, 1 lb. pork flap, 2 pig's tongues, 4 split pig's trotters, 2 pig's ears

2 cucumbers, grated	¼ cup chopped fresh parsley
2 onions grated	1 small hot pepper minced
½ sweet green pepper finely diced	¼ cup water
Fresh limejuice	Salt to taste

Place all meats in a large saucepan, add salt and water to cover, bring to a boil, lower heat and simmer till meats are cooked and very tender- approximately 1½ -2½ hours. Remove meat, wash under cold water and cool. Remove meat from head and cut all meats into bite size pieces, place in a bowl of salted water with ¼ cup limejuice. Refrigerate overnight. Combine the cucumbers, onions, sweet peppers, parsley, hot pepper, more fresh limejuice to taste and ¼ cup water. Drain the meats and pour over the cucumber mixture, let rest for 1-2 hours before serving. Adjust flavour with limejuice and salt to taste. *Cooked breadfruit chunks are often added to the souce.*

This goat stew hails from St Kitts, if young kid is not available mutton or lamb may be substituted but obviously with varying taste to the authentic goat.

Jamaica is also famous for its "MANNISH WATER SOUP" which simmers various meat parts of the goat known as "the fifth quarter" i.e. the head, feet, liver etc. with a variety of ground provisions and green bananas, pumpkin, christophine or chayote, and dumplings. Naturally, ground allspice is added to the seasoning. A humungous amount of this soup is made to feed a crowd and traditionally white rum is served alongside and more than often than not, a bit of the rum is thrown into the soup.

Montserrat serves a similar stew called "GOAT WATER" omitting all provisions.

KIDDIE STEW

¼ cup oil

¼ cup sugar

6 lbs. young goat meat cut up as for stew, salt and pepper to taste

3 chicken or lamb stock cubes dissolved in 6 cups water

4 Tbsps. butter or margarine

1 lb. onions cut into large dice

2 lbs. green papaw, peeled and cut in large dice

1 breadfruit, peeled cored and cut into large dice

6 sprigs each of fresh thyme, marjoram and a small bunch of chives tied together

1 lb. tomatoes chopped

4 Tbsps. tomato ketchup

6 whole cloves

2 whole hot peppers

2 Tbsps. butter

4 Tbsps. flour dissolved in ¼ cup water

Small dumplings - *see recipe in index*

Chopped fresh parsley for garnish

Heat oil and sugar and cook till sugar turns a dark brown colour, be careful not to burn or mixture will be bitter, what you need to achieve is a deep mahogany colour. Now work quickly and add the goat meat pieces, several at a time and cook turning till coated, remove to a large dish and continue cooking the remaining meat. Return all meat to a large boiling pan, add water and stock cubes, bring to a boil, lower heat and simmer goat for 2 hours. In a separate saucepan, heat butter, add onions, fry 3-4 minutes, add papaw and breadfruit and cook stirring 3-4 minutes longer. Add this mixture to the goat. Add tied 'seasonings', tomatoes, ketchup, cloves and hot peppers. Bring to a boil, again lower heat and simmer gently 20-30 minutes till goat is tender, adding more water if required until vegetables are cooked. Increase heat to moderate, add small dumplings, cover and cook 12-15 minutes more. Add flour and water and cook over high heat until thickened. Remove tied seasonings and hot pepper before serving. Sprinkle with chopped parsley.
SERVES 12-16.

Substitute rabbit or lamb for the goat, decreasing the cooking time accordingly as goat is not always readily available. Chicken also makes a wonderful change.

"Limming" (to meet) in the Caribbean

From The Market

Seaside vendors

Seaside hawksters, selling everything from ground provisions to vegetables from their gardens

From The Market

Market Vendors - Invaluable folks they are!

VEGETABLES and STARCHES or "Ground Provisions" as they are known are best purchased in the markets, for it is here that the fresh earthy goodies are to be bought at their prime. Yes, most are now available in our larger supermarkets but they are prepackaged so exact amounts as required cannot be obtained.

It is an experience onto itself to go to Market on Market days, here you can banter for just two tomatoes, six okras, one yam, one bundle of seasonings etc. Here you can touch and feel the firmness of each item you buy. Here you are ensured that the items are freshly reaped that morning.

Not to mention the fun seeing the vendors, chatting and quarrelling amicable, dressed in bright outfits and aprons, with their stalls of wonderful foodstuff all carefully and attractively set out before them.

In many of the photographs accompanying this chapter I have included the actual vegetable or 'Provision'.

I am pleased to see so many vegetable and fruit stands operating as little mini markets springing up all over the island's countryside. To mention one would be Neil at the bottom of GAGG'S HILL who has literally loaned me so many "provisions" for use in the photographs.

Roasting corn on a coalpot

I sometimes add cooked sliced carrots to this for extra eye appeal!
CHRISTOPHENES/CAD IN LIME SAUCE

4 Tbsps. butter
4 christophenes, also known as cad, or chayote - peeled and sliced
3 Tbsps. flour
1 cup milk
Salt and pepper to taste
Juice from ½ lime

Heat butter in a saucepan, when hot, add christophenes and stir-fry 2-3 minutes. Remove from pan and set aside. In same saucepan add flour, cook stirring till mixed in, slowly add milk in a stream stirring constantly, cook till thickened. Add limejuice to taste, salt and pepper to taste. Return christophenes to pan and cook till just heated through. SERVES 4.

Great filling for a good vegetarian roti - see recipe in index
CURRIED CHANNA (CHICK PEAS) AND POTATO

1 cup dry channa, soaked in water to cover overnight
2 Tbsps. oil
1 large onion coarsely chopped
2 garlic cloves minced
2 Tbsps. curry powder
2 potatoes peeled and cut in ½ cubes
1 tomato coarsely chopped
Salt and pepper to taste

Cook channa in unsalted water till tender. Drain reserving 1 cup of the liquid. Heat oil in a saucepan, fry onion 3-4 minutes, add garlic and curry powder, fry 3-4 minutes. Add potatoes and cook stirring till potatoes are coated with curry mixture, add tomato and cook 2-3 minutes longer. Add channa and reserved liquid, salt and pepper to taste. Cover and cook over medium heat 20 minutes or till potatoes are soft. SERVES 4-6.

ROAST AND BOILED CORN

TO ROAST CORN:

EITHER... Remove husks and silk from corn, place on coalpot or barbecue directly on grills and cook turning frequently for 10-12 minutes or till charred.

OR........... Gently slide back husks leaving them on the ear of corn, remove silk, dot with salt and peppered butter, carefully return husks to original position and grill turning often for 10-15 minutes.

TO BOIL CORN:

EITHER ... Cook a piece of salted pigtail or salt beef in about 6 cups of water with some chopped hot pepper and the cleaned husks from the corn for 30 minutes. Add husked corn and simmer 8-10 minutes.

OR….......... Bring 1 cup milk with 2 Tbsps. sugar to a boil, add husked corn and simmer till tender.

SQUASH

12 baby squash
2 Tbsps. butter
Juice from ½ a lime
2 Tbsps. chopped parsley
Salt and pepper to taste
Cut tips off squash and cut in half lengthways. Heat butter and lime juice in a saucepan, add squash and cook 3-4 minutes. Salt and pepper to taste, sprinkle with parsley. SERVES 4.

DHAL

1 package dried yellow split peas
2 onions chopped
2 cloves garlic minced
1 tsp. cumin seed
2 Tbsps. curry powder
Small piece hot pepper minced
Salt and pepper to taste
Boil the peas in unsalted water to cover till very soft, about 30-40 minutes. In a separate pan heat some oil and fry the onion for 5 minutes, add garlic, cumin, curry, hot pepper and fry for 2-3 minutes longer, add the peas with some of the liquid and cook mashing the peas on the side of the pan till the mixture is thick and pureed with some lumps of peas left. Salt and pepper to taste. SERVES 6.

OKRA SLUSH

2 Tbsps. butter
1 each onion and garlic chopped coarsely
12 okras, washed and sliced ¼" thick
4 tomatoes chopped coarsely
¼ cup chicken or beef stock
Salt and pepper to taste
Heat butter in a frying pan, add onions and cook 3-4 minutes, add garlic and okra and fry turning and quoting with onion mixture, add tomatoes and stock, salt and pepper to taste. Cover and cook 10 minutes over low heat. Sometimes a tin of drained corn is added. SERVES 4-6.

FRESH DOVED PIDGEON PEAS (See recipe for pigeon peas and rice *in index*. Follow instructions for preparing the peas but omit rice and add small amounts of water at a time, cooking till peas are soft and a sauce is formed)

CORN PIE *(my sister Brenda's recipe, she prepares this every Christmas)*

2 eggs well beaten
⅔ cup milk
3 Tbsps. butter melted
1x16oz. tin creamed corn
½ cup flour
1 Tbsp. sugar
Combine all ingredients, place in greased casserole dish. Bake in a 350F Oven for 50-60 minutes or till set. SERVES 6.

Curried Split Pea Dhal

Okra Slush

Pickled green Bananas

OKRA GUMBO

2 Tbsps. butter
1 Tbsp. olive oil
1 large onion chopped
1 garlic clove minced
½ lb. okras sliced ½" thick
16 oz. tin tomatoes coarsely chopped, drained, liquid reserved
1 Tbsp. chopped fresh thyme
¼ cup freshly chopped parsley
¼ cup freshly chopped chives
Small piece hot pepper minced.
Dash of Worcestershire sauce
Heat butter and oil in a large saucepan, add onions and fry 4-5 minutes, add garlic and cook 2 minutes more, add okras and cook stirring till okras are coated with onion mixture, add tomatoes, thyme, parsley, chives, hot pepper and Worcestershire. Cook 2-3 minutes. Add reserved tomato liquid, salt and pepper to taste and cook over moderate heat till liquid has mostly evaporated and okras are cooked. *Cooked crab, fish, shrimp or chicken or a combination of all may be added at the end*. SERVES 4-6.

PUMPKIN CASSEROLE

3 lbs. pumpkin, peeled and cut into 2" slices
3 Tbsps. butter
Salt and pepper to taste
Buttered crumbs
Steam pumpkin over boiling water till tender. Mash with butter, salt and pepper, place in buttered casserole dish, top with buttered breadcrumbs and bake in a preheated 375.F Oven for 25 minutes. SERVES 6.

BAKED PUMPKIN

Cut pumpkin into large 3-4"cubes, retaining skin. Place in buttered baking pan. Dot with butter, salt and pepper. Bake 375F oven for 30-40 minutes.

SEE ALSO RECIPE FOR PUMPKIN FRITTERS - *see index*

BANANAS GREEN-PICKLED or SOUSED

8 green bananas in their skins
1 small cucumber, grated
1 small onion grated
1 Tbsp. chopped parsley
Small piece of hot pepper minced
Juice of 1 lime
Salt to taste.
Boil bananas in their skins till soft, about 20 minutes. Remove skins and cut in 3-4 pieces place in dish with other ingredients. Let sit at least 1 hour or longer before serving. SERVES 4.

HOT PICKLED GREEN BANANAS

Cook and prepare green bananas as above. toss with bay sauce instead of pickle - *see index.*

FOO FOO *(Plantain Balls, also spelt as FOU FOU) - TRINIDAD and BARBADOS*
5 green plantains
Salt to taste
Water
Cook plantains in unsalted water to cover for 30 minutes or till soft and tender. Peel, chop coarsely and pound in a mortar and pestle until smooth, keep dipping the pestle in water to avoid it sticking. Season with salt and form into small balls. *Serve with soups or stews.* SERVES 4.

BACON WRAPPED PLANTAIN
2 plantains
4 bacon rashers cut in half
Peel plantains and cut into 2" thick slices, wrap in slice of bacon, secure with toothpicks and bake in a preheated 375F. Oven for 30 minutes. SERVES 4.

Fried plantain accompanies most meals. Sometimes it is sliced into ¼" slices vertically, fried and sprinkled with sugar while still hot.
FRIED PLANTAIN
3-4 very ripe plantains
Shallow oil for frying
Peel plantains, slice each horizontally into 5-6 slices. Heat oil and fry plantain till golden, Drain on kitchen paper and serve. SERVES 4. *(Not when my father is present, he liked these with every meal.)*

BAKED WHOLE PLANTAIN
3 peeled whole ripe plantains
3 Tbsps. butter
3 Tbsps. brown sugar
Ground cinnamon
Place plantains in a well buttered dish. Dot each with softened butter, sprinkle each with 1 Tbsp. sugar and dust each lightly with cinnamon. Bake in a preheated 375.F. Oven 20-30 minutes. SERVES 6.

SCALLOPED PLANTAIN
Follow above recipe but slice the plantains and keep layering till all are used.

VEGETABLE COOK-UP
½ lb. cristophenes
½ lb. carrots
½ lb. cabbage
½ lb. tomatoes
1 onion sliced
1 each red yellow and green sweet peppers sliced
Grated ginger
Pinch of sugar
3 Tbsps. butter
Salt and pepper to taste
Chop tomatoes, cut remaining vegetables into julienne strips, mix with ginger, sugar and salt and pepper to taste. Steam vegetables till cooked, add butter and mix in. SERVES 6.

Baked whole and Fried Plantains

Creamed Callaloo

CREAMED CALLALOO

1 Tbsp. butter
1 large onion minced
2 garlic cloves minced
Small piece hot pepper minced
Sprig fresh thyme
½ lb. ocroes, sliced thin
1 ½ lbs. callaloo or dasheen leaves chopped
¼ cup chicken stock
¾ cup coconut milk
¼ tsp. freshly grated nutmeg
Salt and pepper to taste

Heat butter in a saucepan, add onion and fry 4-5 minutes. Add garlic, hot pepper and thyme, fry 2-3 minutes. Add okras and fry 2 minutes. Add callaloo and pour over the stock and coconut milk. Bring to a boil, add nutmeg, salt and pepper to taste. Lower heat and simmer covered 20-25 minutes or till liquid is absorbed. Remove sprig of thyme before serving. SERVES 6-8.

ACKEE CURRIED

8-10 fresh Jamaican ackee pods, cleaned, prepared to eat and boiled for 5 minutes or 2 tin ackees
1 cup coconut milk
Salt and pepper to taste
2 Tbsps. flour
1 Tbsp. curry powder
¼ tsp. cumin seed
2 Tbsps. butter
Juice of small lime

Heat butter in heavy saucepan, add curry powder and cumin seed and cook over medium heat for two minutes. Add flour and cook one minute longer, slowly add coconut milk, stirring continuously until beginning to thicken. Add ackees, reduce heat and simmer slowly till most of the sauce is absorbed. Season with salt and pepper to taste and sprinkle with limejuice just before serving. SERVES 6.

AUBERGINE IN COCONUT CREAM

2 aubergines (eggplants) sliced, skin left on
¼ cup sweet oil (Olive oil)
2 onions sliced thin
2 garlic cloves sliced thin
6 tomatoes chopped
1 cup coconut milk
½ tsp. curry powder
Salt and pepper to taste

Salt eggplant slices, place in a colander for 30 minutes, rinse and pat dry. Heat oil in a large frying pan, cook eggplant in batches in a single layer turning once till golden. As eggplant cooks, place in a casserole dish in layers, salt and peppering between layers. When eggplants are cooked, add onions to the oil, additional oil may be needed, fry for a few minutes till soft and barely golden, add curry powder and garlic and cook 2 minutes more, add tomato, coconut milk and cook stirring occasionally for 10 minutes. Pour hot mixture over the eggplant, cover with foil and bake in a preheated 325F Oven for 40 minutes. SERVES 6.

From The Market

BAKED WHOLE SWEET POTATOES
4 small sweet potatoes, scrubbed and pricked with a skewer.
Bake sweet potatoes in a 400F oven for 45 minutes to 1 hour or till test done when pierced with a skewer. Serve with lots of butter, salt and pepper. SERVES 4.

GRILLED SWEET POTATOES
Boil sweet potatoes till cooked, cool. Peel, slice thickly, brush with butter and grill.

CANDIED SWEET POTATOES
4 medium sweet potatoes, boiled in their skins, cooled, peeled and sliced into ½" rounds or cubes
¼ cup butter
½ cup brown sugar
¼ cup water
Dash ground cinnamon and grated fresh nutmeg
In a frying pan, make a syrup by combining butter, sugar, water and spices. Add the sliced sweet potatoes and cook turning till quoted and heated through. SERVES 4-6.

ORANGE SWEET POTATOES
4 small sweet potatoes, boiled in their skins till tender but firm
½ cup sugar
2 Tbsps. rum
¼ cup butter
½ cup fresh orange juice
2 Tbsps. orange marmalade
Peel and slice potatoes into ½" slices. Melt butter in a small saucepan, add sugar, rum, orange juice and marmalade, cook till sugar dissolves. Toss with sliced sweet potatoes and place in a buttered dish. Broil, turning slices till golden brown. SERVES 4.

PINEAPPLE SWEET POTATOES
3 lbs. peeled, boiled sweet potatoes
¼ cup brown sugar
Salt and pepper to taste
½ cup butter
1 cup drained crushed pineapple, reserve liquid
Mash sweet potatoes with the reserved pineapple liquid, half of the butter and salt and pepper to taste. Fold in the pineapple, place mixture in a buttered dish, dot with remaining butter, sprinkle with the sugar and bake in a preheated 400F. Oven for 20 minutes. SERVES 6-8.

CASSAVA FRIED *(Cassava, known as Yuca, available in Latin American markets)*
Peel and boil cassava in salted water till tender. Cool, remove center cord, dredge in flour and deep fat fry.

CASSAVA CHIPS
Peel cassava, slice into paper - thin rounds, deep fat fry. Drain on kitchen paper. Sprinkle with salt to serve.

CASSAVA PATTIES - Boil cassava as above, remove center core and mash, to every cup of cassava add 1 beaten egg, ½ tsp. baking powder, 1 chive chopped, salt and lots of black pepper. Shape into patties, coat well with dried breadcrumbs. Fry in shallow hot oil.

Front - Candied Sweet Potatoes, Baked whole Sweet Potatoes, Back - Grilled Sweet Potatoes

Cassava Patties

Buttered herbed breadfruit

From The Market

Grenada is famous for its "Oildown", sometimes callaloo/dasheen leaves are added.

BREADFRUIT OILDOWN

½ lb. salted pigtail or salt beef cut in 2" pieces and soaked overnight
1 breadfruit peeled, cored and cut into 2" pieces
1 hot pepper left whole
2 onions chopped
1 small bunch chives chopped
1 clove of garlic minced
Fresh sprigs of thyme, parsley and celery stalk tied together
5 cups coconut milk
2 Tbsps. curry powder plus 1 Tbsp. fresh chopped coriander leaves or chadon bene, optional.
Boil salt meat in water till tender. Add all remaining ingredients in order listed and cook at a bare simmer for 45 minutes to 1 hour or until most but not all of the liquid is absorbed. Remove whole pepper, sprigs of herbs and serve. SERVES 6.

BREADFRUIT BALLS *(An excellent way to use left over cooked breadfruit or cou cou. We often serve these in our restaurant)*

2 cups cooked mashed breadfruit
1 egg beaten
3 chopped chives
½ onion grated
¼ cup flour
1 rounded tsp. baking powder
Milk to bind
Salt and pepper to taste
Combine all ingredients in a bowl and mix well. Fry in deep hot fat by large teaspoonfulls till golden. Serve immediately. SERVES 8.

SCALLOPED BREADFRUIT

½ breadfruit, peeled, cored and boiled in salted water till tender but firm
4 rashers bacon cut into 1" lengths
3 Tbsps. butter
1 large onion sliced thin
3 Tbsps. flour
3 cups milk
1 cup grated cheddar cheese
Freshly grated nutmeg
Salt and pepper to taste.
Slice breadfruit into long thin slices, set aside. Cook bacon in large saucepan till soft and some of the fat is rendered. Remove bacon and set aside. Add butter and onion to saucepan with the bacon fat, cook till onion is soft. Add flour and cook till incorporated. Slowly add milk, stirring constantly till mixture thickens slightly. Add cheese, nutmeg salt and pepper to taste. In a casserole dish, lawyer ⅓ breadfruit, ½ of reserved bacon, then ⅓ cheese sauce. Continue layering as mentioned. Bake in a preheated 350F. Oven for 20-25 minutes or till bubbly. SERVES 6.

BUTTERED HERBED BREADFRUIT:
Peel, core, slice breadfruit and boil in salted water to cover. Drain and dot with butter, salt and pepper and chopped chives.

BREADFRUIT SALAD

1 small breadfruit, cored, peeled and boiled in salted water till firm but cooked
1 cup cooked firm carrots, diced
1 cup green peas, cooked till still firm
1 stalk of celery chopped
1 onion grated
½ cup parsley minced
4 blades of chive chopped
½ cup mayonnaise
Juice from ½ a lime
Salt and pepper to taste
4 hard-boiled eggs sliced

Dice breadfruit into ½" chunks. Add carrots, green peas, celery, onion, parsley and chives. Mix mayonnaise with lime-juice, gently fold into breadfruit mixture, salt and pepper to taste and if necessary add a little more mayonnaise and limejuice to taste. Garnish dish with eggs slices. SERVES 6.

STUFFED BACK BREADFRUIT

1 whole breadfruit unpeeled
Salted water to cover
1 cup milk
¼ cup butter
1 egg lightly beaten
Salt and pepper to taste
Grated cheddar cheese

Cook whole breadfruit in water till tender about 40 minutes. Cool slightly, cut in half lengthways and carefully cut out core and discard, now carefully remove flesh from breadfruit leaving a ½" wall, reserve shell. Mash flesh with butter, milk and fold in the egg. Salt and pepper to taste. Return mixture to shell. Sprinkle with grated cheese and bake in a 375F. Oven for 30 minutes. SERVES 8.

BREADNUT *(also known as Chataigne. Break up breadnut in half. Remove seeds and clean of any flesh adhering to it. Boil seeds in salted water till tender. Remove skin from nuts)*

RECIPE 1: Sprinkle with salt and serve. I would eat these by the handfuls as a child.

RECIPE 2: Follow recipe for Curried Channa, substituting prepared breadnuts.

RECIPE 3: Use in any Stuffing recipe that calls for Chestnuts. *Excellent stuffing for turkey or chicken.*

RECIPE 4: Mash with a little grated onion, butter, milk and salt and pepper to taste.

RECIPE 5: Add prepared breadnuts to soups or stews.

RECIPE 6: Mash 2 cups cooked breadnuts: combine with 1 egg beaten, 3 tsps. chopped seasoning (chive, parsley, hot pepper, salt and pepper),1 cup flour with a little milk to bind. Fry till by teaspoonfulls till golden.

Stuffed Back Breadfruit

Breadnuts in raw, peeled and cooked stages

Cou Cous - Top: Corn Meal,   Right: Green banana,   Left: Breadfruit

COU COU's are descendant from our African heritage, although made famous and probably eaten more in Barbados than the other islands, some form of COU COU is to be found everywhere. A special "COU COU stick" is used for making of Cou Cous in Barbados but any wooden spoon will do. Here are a few versions from around the Caribbean.

CORN MEAL COU COU

12 okras, sliced thin

3 cups cornmeal

6-8 cups water

2 tsps. salt

2 Tbsps. butter, preferably red butter (Irish cooking butter)

Bring water to a boil, add okras and salt and cook till very soft and mushy. Use some of the pan liquid to moisten the cornmeal. Place about half of the okra liquid in another pan, add the cornmeal slowly, turning with a cou cou stick and adding more okra liquid as needed and stirring continuosly. When mixture is smooth and stiff, add the butter. Cover and let steam over very low heat for a few minutes. Turn out into a buttered pudding basin. ***Traditionally served in Barbados as it's National dish with stewed salt fish or steamed flying fish. What is an absolute necessity is to serve this with lots of gravy.*** SERVES 6.

CORN COU COU (*Grenada*)

Omit okras and use a combination of 3 cups of freshly made coconut milk with 2-3 cups of water.

CORN COU COU WITH FISH

Omit okras and fry 3-4 slices of bacon with a little minced hot pepper and the water, add cornmeal and cook as above. Stir in 1 lb. cooked flaked salt fish, reheat and serve.

CORN COU COU (*Tobago origin*) Follow recipe for CORNMEAL cou cou but use chicken stock instead of water.

CORN COU COU WITH CORN (*Trinidad origin*) Make CORNMEAL cou cou and add

¾ lb. grated fresh corn to the liquid.

BREADFRUIT COU-COU

1 salted pigtail or ¼ lb. salted beef soaked overnight.

1 breadfruit, cored and peeled

1 onion chopped

3 sprigs of fresh thyme chopped

3 Tbsps. butter

Boil salt meat in 6 cups water till tender, about 45 minutes. Cut breadfruit in small thick slices, add to pot with onion and thyme and continue boiling till breadfruit is very soft. Remove breadfruit from pot reserving liquid and mash adding reserved liquid. Remove meat from bones and fold into the breadfruit. Place in a bowl and top butter, preferably red or salted butter. SERVES 8.

GREEN BANANA COU COU

Piece of salted pigtail or beef, soaked overnight in water to cover

1 hand green bananas

Small piece hot pepper minced

1 onion chopped

2 Tbsps. butter

Cook salted meat in water with hot pepper and onion to cover till tender, about 1 hour. Add peeled sliced green bananas and cook till mushy about 20 minutes. Remove meat from bones and reserve. Drain the bananas, reserving the liquid, and mash using some of the reserved liquid, fold in the meat, salt and pepper to taste and the butter. SERVES 4-6.

YAM BALLS or CROQUETTES

2 cups cooked mashed yam, salt and pepper to taste
½ onion grated
½ cup flour
2 eggs beaten
1 cup dry breadcrumbs
Mix yam with onion, salt and pepper to taste. Form into balls or cylinder shapes, roll in flour, then eggs and coat completely with breadcrumbs. Fry in oil till hot and golden. MAKES 16.

YAM-STUFFED BACK

1 large whole baking yam with skin, scrubbed
Butter, milk, salt and pepper to taste.
1 cup grated cheddar cheese
Bake yam in a hot 400F. Oven for 1 hour or till skewer inserted in center test done. Cut yam in half lengthways and carefully scoop out the flesh leaving skin intact. Mash with butter, milk, salt and pepper. Fold in half the cheese. Return to the shell, cover top with remaining cheese and bake or broil till top is golden and cheese melted. SERVES 4-6.

YAM CHIPS

Cook peeled yam till firm but cooked. Cut into chip sizes and deep fat fry.

BAJAN EDDOES

12 eddoes in their skins
Juice of 2-3 limes
3 Tbsps. red salted butter or plain butter
1 onion chopped fine
Small piece hot pepper minced
Salt to taste
Wash, scrub and cook eddoes in water till tender. Peel and while warm, add the limejuice, butter, onion, pepper, and salt to taste. Top with ¼-½ cup hot water and mix. SERVES 4.

MASHED TANNIAS

8 tannias peeled and sliced
2 Tbsps. butter
¼ cup. milk
3 chives chopped
Salt and lots of black pepper to taste
(Optional, buttered breadcrumbs)
Boil tannias in salted water till tender. Drain and mash with butter, milk, salt and pepper. Fold in the chives and serve immediately. Or, place in buttered dish, top with buttered crumbs and bake in a preheated 375F. Oven for 20-25 minutes. SERVES 4.

FRIED EDDOES

12 eddoes
Oil for deep fat frying
Boil eddoes in their skins till soft 16-20 minutes. Cool slightly, peel leaving eddoes whole and deep fat fry till golden. SERVES 4.

YAM, stuffed back and YAM chips, my daughter Laura's and husband's favourite, the two love the earthy taste of the yam skin

Bajan Eddoes

Caribbean Rice - Bottom: Pigeon peas & Rice, Middle: Jamaican Rice & Peas, Top: Channa & Rice

Notice the difference- in Jamaica it is "Rice and Peas", yet throughout the other islands it is mainly known as "Peas and Rice".

JAMAICAN RICE AND PEAS

½ lb. dried red kidney beans, soaked in water to cover overnight

2 Tbsps. butter or bacon fat

3 sprigs fresh thyme chopped

½ a red hot pepper minced

4 chives chopped

2 onions chopped

2 garlic cloves minced

4 cups coconut milk

2 cups raw rice

2 tsps. salt

1 cup water

Heat butter or bacon fat in a large saucepan, fry thyme, hot pepper, chives, onion and garlic 2-3 minutes. Add beans and coconut milk. Bring to a boil, lower heat and cook covered till beans are tender but still firm-about 1 hour. Add rice, salt and water, bring to a boil again, lower heat and cook covered 20-25 minutes or till rice is cooked and liquid absorbed. SERVES 6.

PIGEON PEAS AND RICE

1 cup dry pigeon peas, soaked overnight

1 salted pigtail or piece of salt beef,

5 cups water

3 Tbsps. butter

1 onion

2 garlic cloves minced

3 sprigs each fresh thyme and marjoram chopped fine

¼ a hot red pepper minced

1 Tbsp. Worcestershire sauce

2 cups rice

Place meat in water and bring to a boil. Cook till meat is tender, about 2 hours, add dried peas and continue cooking till peas are cooked but still firm- 45minutes to 1 hour. Drain peas reserving liquid. In a separate saucepan heat butter, fry onion, clove, garlic, thyme, marjoram and hot pepper. Measure reserved liquid and add enough water to make bring the level to 4 ¼ cups, add this to the pan along with the reserved peas, rice and Worcestershire. Bring to a boil, lower heat and cook covered till liquid is absorbed and rice is cooked, about 20-25 minutes. SERVES 6-8.

VARIATIONS

: **BLACK EYE PEAS AND RICE:** Cook as above using black eye peas with the addition of cut up pork flap.

: **FIELD PEAS AND RICE:** Cook as above using field peas.

: **CHANNA (CHICK PEAS) AND RICE:** Cook as above using Channa but omit Worcestershire sauce and replace with 1 Tbsp. curry powder.

: **SPLIT PEAS AND RICE:** Cook as for Channa.

: **BLACK BEANS AND RICE:** Cook as per pigeon peas using black beans, add 1 Tbsp. sugar.

Diced cooked chicken or pork or shrimp or a combination of all may be added.

CARIBBEAN CHINESE FRIED RICE

4 Tbsps. oil
4 slices bacon, diced
2 slices ham cut julienne
1 large onion chopped
4 blades chive chopped
1 each sweet pepper and celery stalk chopped
2 carrots coarsely grated
4 cups cooked plain rice
2 Tbsps. soy sauce
½ tsp. hot pepper sauce

Heat oil, fry bacon till translucent, add ham, onion, chive, sweet pepper, celery and carrots: stir fry a few minutes, add rice by large spoonfuls and continue stir frying, add hot sauce, and soy sauce to taste. Continue stirring till rice is heated. SERVES 6.

COCONUT RICE

1 cup raw rice
1 garlic clove minced
1 Tbsp. butter
½ cup chopped chives
½ cup chopped green sweet peppers
Small piece hot pepper minced
2 cups coconut milk plus ½ cup water
1 tsp. salt

Heat butter in medium saucepan, add rice and cook stirring till quoted with butter, add garlic, chives, sweet peppers, hot pepper and salt. Add coconut milk and water, bring to a boil, lower heat, cover and cook for 20-25 minutes or till liquid is absorbed and rice cooked. SERVES 4.

CURRIED RICE:
To above recipe, fry 1 chopped onion, 1 Tbsp. curry powder and ½ tsp. whole cumin seeds with the herbs, continue as per recipe above.

OKRA AND RICE

2 Tbsps. butter
24 okras sliced
2 garlic cloves minced
1 onion chopped
Piece soaked cooked salted meat or salted fish
2 sprigs fresh thyme chopped
2 cups rice
Salt to taste
4½ cups water or half water and half coconut milk

Heat butter in a saucepan, add okras, garlic and onion, fry 3-4 minutes, add salted meat or fish and thyme fry 2-3 minutes. Add rice, fry 1 minute. Add liquid, adjust for salt, bring to a boil, lower heat and cook covered till rice is cooked and liquid absorbed. SERVES 6.

Caribbean Chinese fried rice

Okra and rice

From The Market

Caribbean avocadoes off my tree

This is a sauce that I grew up with, although served as a side sauce I found that marinating fish, chicken, pork and beef prior to grilling both enhanced and tenderized my end product. I make this in avocado season and freeze it for marinating purposes when needed.

AVOCADO GUASACACA

½ lb. each fresh parsley, cilantro and onions
1 lb. avocado flesh, pealed and seeded
2 cups corn oil
¼ cup vinegar
½ Tbsp. salt
6 garlic cloves minced
Black pepper to taste
Mince or chop all ingredients together in blender or food processor till coarsely chopped.

AVOCADO AND LIME SALSA

1 firm ripe avocado, peeled and diced
1 bunch chopped chives
2 Tbsps. olive oil
Juice from 1 fresh lime
Small piece hot pepper minced
1 tomato chopped
Combine all ingredients and toss lightly. MAKES ABOUT 1 CUP.

This recipe is wonderful served over a bed of lettuce and topped with boiled, chilled shrimp.

AVOCADO MOLD

1 pkg. unflavoured gelatin dissolved in 4 Tbsps. water
¼ of an onion, peeled
1 large avocado, pealed, seeded and sliced
1 Tbsp. fresh limejuice
Dash of cayenne pepper
2 Tbsps. chopped fresh coriander (cilantro) or 2 sprigs chadon bene
2 blades of chive chopped
Salt and pepper to taste
½ cup cream
Heat gelatin over gentle flame to dissolve or microwave 20 seconds, set aside to cool. In food processor, process onion 2-3 seconds, add avocado, limejuice, cayenne, coriander, and chives, process 4-5 seconds. Add gelatin mixture and cream and process 2-3 seconds more. Pour into a greased mold and refrigerate till set. Unmold to serve and garnish with cilantro leaves. SERVES 8. *Make these into small individual molds, top with shrimp for a great starter.*

This is my father-in-law's favourite way to eat an avocado.

FATHER IN-LAW'S AVOCADO

Top peeled avocado slices with a dash of Worcestershire sauce and fresh limejuice.
TIPS:to prepare avocado dishes in advance, <u>retain the seed</u> and place seed over avocado to stop discolouration.
: a squeeze of fresh limejuice over slices also helps to stop discolouration.
:TO FREEZE avocado, cut into large thick slices and coated thoroughly with about a ¼ cup of fresh lime juice, lay slices side by side flat and freeze in freezer bags. Use in dips or sauces.

A totally Bajan dish served at Christmas time. Legend has it that the Scottish settlers created it with local produce in an attempt to reproduce their famous "haggis".

JUG JUG

½ lb. salt beef or pigtail soaked in water to cover overnight

½ lb. fresh pork

8 cups pigeon peas

Small piece of hot pepper minced

3 large onions chopped

1 bunch chives chopped

3 Tbsps. fresh thyme

1 tsp. fresh marjoram

3 Tbsps. butter

½ cup guinea corn flour

Salt and pepper to taste

Cook meats in water till soft, add peas and all remaining ingredients except butter and guinea corn flour and cook till peas are tender and very soft. Drain peas reserving the stock. Remove meat from bones. Grind the peas and meat and return to the pan. Mix the guinea corn flour with some of the pea stock and mix into the pea mixture, cook stirring till mixture thickens adding more stock as needed for approximately 20 minutes. Stir in butter just before serving. Salt and pepper to taste.

SERVES 12.

Macaroni pie appears with every stewed dish and is often just bought and eaten by itself with lots of hot pepper sauce poured over. Simply ask for PIE and it will mean this dish.

MACARONI PIE *(cut the macaroni into pieces before cooking in lots of salted boiling water)*

½ lb. cooked macaroni

4 Tbsps. butter

4 Tbsps. flour

1 onion finely chopped

2 eggs lightly beaten

1 cup milk

Dash of hot pepper sauce

½ cup grated cheddar cheese for sauce plus additional for topping

Heat butter in a saucepan, add flour and cook 1 minute, add onion and milk stirring continuously till mixture thickens, cool slightly, add salt and pepper to taste, dash of hot sauce, and cheese. Mix with macaroni, place in a greased casserole dish, top with additional grated cheddar and bake in a preheated 375.F. Oven for 30 minutes. SERVES 6.

ALTERNATIVE METHOD FOR MACARONI PIE

To ½ lb. cooked macaroni as above - ADD:

½ lb. grated cheddar cheese plus additional for topping

1 onion grated

1 small sweet pepper grated

2 eggs beaten with 1 cup of milk

¼ cup flour

¼ cup ketchup

Dash of hot pepper sauce

Combine all ingredients, place in greased casserole dish. Top with additional grated cheddar cheese. Bake in a 350.F. Oven till golden and cooked 30-40 minutes. SERVES 6.

Two scenes from Tobago

Fishing off a groyne

Caribbean fish

Catch Of The Day

Fish market - A hive of activity

Janette doing what she does best

A visit to any fish market in the Caribbean is a must. The display and variety of fish is something to behold but what makes it so special is the boisterousness of the fish vendors, the business of the whole scene, not to mention the colourful language. Sometimes it is best that we do not understand their special language! I love to go and talk to these folk and have learnt so much from them through the years as to how to cook and prepare fish for maximum flavour and texture.

Our fishermen/women are a Nation on to themselves. I salute them all, for the wonderful job they are doing and more than anything for the end result of their labours. FISH! GLORIOUS FISH!!!

We consume volumes of fish in the Caribbean and besides our tried and true recipes we are now preparing fish in so many varied ways that a book could be written on this alone.

For many of you who live abroad and may not be able to obtain our species of fish, simply substitute the closest in shape and size and prepare it as we do in the Caribbean, the results will be as nostalgic as you can get to the real 'mccoy'.

One serious bit of advice is to befriend a fisherfolk, I have done so with Janette Squires, who spoils me by letting me know when certain fish are plentiful and at cheaper prices, by somehow always managing to locate a specific type of fish for me when no one else can and by specially gutting and cleaning my fish exactly how I like it. Thanks Janette!

Catch Of The Day

Boiled lobster in Caribbean sea water

Catch Of The Day

Lobsters found in the Caribbean are the spiny variety available between December and April.

The ultimate way to cook lobster. Sorry it is very important to use Caribbean Sea water… no other seasoning is added or necessary. For a really simple dish, boil extra live lobsters. Use to make salads - see recipe below, or casseroles.

BOILED LOBSTER

Large pot of Caribbean Sea water
2-4 live lobsters
Bring seawater to the boil. Plunge lobsters in head first and cover quickly holding the cover down for a few minutes. Boil vigorously for 5 minutes for small lobsters. Turn off heat and leave for 5 minutes. Remove from water and let sit for 5 minutes. Add a few extra minutes for medium in the process and a few extra again for larger lobsters. Split lobster in half from head to tail. Rinse out entrails in head and serve. SERVES 2-4.
At my restaurant I fill the lobster head cavity with a colourful seasoned rice and serve it with atleast 3 or 4 dipping sauces, so from one lobster meal you get many tantalizing flavours. Here are the basic four sauces I use.

GARLIC BUTTER: Serve with warmed garlic butter from grilled lobster recipe below.

CARIBBEAN MAYONNAISE SAUCE: Combine 1 cup mayonnaise with ¼ cup each of chopped chives, parsley and juice from ½ to 1 lime according to taste.

COVE CHUTNEY MAYO: Combine ½ cup mayonnaise with 1 tsp. curry powder and 2 Tbsps. Caribbean mango chutney.

QUICK SEAFOOD DIP: Combine ½ cup ketchup with ¼ cup mayonnaise, juice from ½ a lime plus a dash of Worcestershire sauce.

LOBSTER SALAD

Cooked lobster. Cut lobster meat into pieces, coat with one of the mayonnaises above, add chopped chive, cooked diced carrot and cooked green peas. Serve over a bed of lettuce, garnished with tomato wedges and cucumber slices.

GRILLED or BROILED LOBSTER TAILS

2 lobsters tails, slit down the hard shell and opened slightly
Juice from 1 lime
¼ lb. butter, softened
1 Tbsp. chopped chives
1 Tbsp. chopped parsley
1 garlic clove minced
Tiny piece of hot pepper minced or a dash of dried mustard powder
Salt and pepper to taste
Whip butter, chives, parsley, garlic, hot pepper or mustard and limejuice. Salt and pepper exposed flesh of lobster. Heat grill or BBQ. Baste tails with butter mixture and place open or cut side down on grill. Cook 3-4 minutes, turn and continue cooking 2-3 minutes, turn again and baste with butter mixture again and cook 3-4 minutes or till cooked. Serve with remaining butter slightly warmed or with Caribbean mayonnaise sauce - *see recipe above.* SERVES 2.

HOT AND SPICY FRIED SHRIMP

1 lb. shrimp, shelled and deveined
Salt and pepper to taste
½ cup flour
½ cup beer
1 Tbsp. hot pepper sauce
2 Tbsps. prepared "Seasoning"- *see recipe in index*
¼ tsp. baking soda
Pinch of baking powder
Oil for deep-frying
Lime wedges for serving

Salt and pepper shrimp, set aside. Whisk flour, beer, hot sauce, "seasoning", baking soda and baking powder till lump free. Heat oil, dip shrimp in batter and fry till golden. Serve with lime wedges. SERVES 4. *(Only serves 2 if it is I eating them!).*

CURRIED SHRIMP *(Try this also by adding a bit of sherry at the end)*

1 lb. shrimp, shelled and deveined
Salt and pepper to taste
3 Tbsps. butter or oil
1 Tbsp. curry powder
1 tsp. ground cumin
1 large onion chopped
½ hot pepper minced
1 celery stalk chopped fine
2 garlic cloves minced
1 Tbsp. flour
1 cup water

Salt and pepper shrimp. Heat butter or oil in a frying pan, fry shrimp turning for 1 minute, remove from pan and set aside. To the same pan add curry powder, cumin, onion, hot pepper, celery and garlic, fry 2-3 minutes. Add flour and cook 1 minute. Add water and cook stirring till mixture begins to thicken. Return shrimp to pan, lower heat and simmer 2-3 minutes longer. SERVES 4. *To use as a filler for rotis, add 1 large peeled diced potato with the water, boil till tender then return shrimp to saucepan and cook till just heated through.*

GRILLED SHRIMP

2 lbs. extra large shrimp peeled and deveined
Salt and pepper to taste
1 cup melted butter
4 garlic cloves minced
1 hot pepper minced
Juice from 1 lime
¼ cup chopped fresh basil or chives or parsley

Salt and pepper shrimp, thread on skewers if liked. Combine melted butter with garlic, hot pepper, limejuice and herb of choice. Baste the shrimp with the butter mixture and grill or BBQ turning and basting often 3-5 minutes or till cooked. Garnish with the same herb used in the butter mixture. Serve with remaining butter sauce. SERVES 6.

Hot & Spicy Shrimp

Grilled Shrimp

Shrimp in garlic sauce

SHRIMP IN WEST INDIAN CREOLE SAUCE *(Add 12 okra with the onions if preferred)*

1 lb. shrimp, shelled and deveined
Salt and black pepper to taste
2 Tbsps. butter
1 each large onion, sweet pepper and garlic clove chopped
3 blades chive chopped
2 celery ribs coarsely chopped
Small piece hot pepper minced
1 tin (16ozs.) tomatoes, drained and coarsely chopped, reserve liquid
Dash of ground clove
1 Tbsp. each fresh minced thyme and parsley
1 Tbsp. prepared chili powder
Additional chopped parsley for garnishing

Salt and pepper shrimp. Heat butter in frying pan, add shrimp and cook 1-2 minutes, remove from pan and set aside. In same pan, fry the onion, sweet pepper, garlic, chive, celery and hot pepper for 2-3 minutes. Add tomatoes, clove, thyme, parsley and chili powder, cook till vegetables are soft, add reserved tomato liquid and cook till mixture thickens, about 10 minutes. Return shrimp to pan, and continue cooking over low heat till shrimp are heated through,2-3 minutes. Garnish with lots of chopped parsley. *Serve over a bed of fluffy rice, accompanied by crisp cooked okras.* SERVES 4.

Flouring the shrimp helps retain the garlic flavour on each morsel.

SHRIMP IN GARLIC SAUCE

1 lb. shrimp, shelled and deveined
Salt and pepper to taste
Flour to dredge shrimp
2 garlic cloves minced
¼ cup butter softened
3 Tbsps. each chopped chives and parsley
Juice from ½ a lime

Salt and pepper shrimp, dredge lightly in flour. Heat 2 Tbsps. of the butter, fry shrimp 2 minutes, remove from pan. To the same pan add garlic and remaining butter and cook over a low flame till butter is just beginning to turn to liquid, just a few seconds, add chives and parsley, return shrimp and cook tossing till shrimp are coated with butter mixture and heated through, about 2 minutes. Sprinkle with limejuice to serve. SERVES 4.

SHRIMP IN EGG WHITE SAUCE *(Trinidad Chinese origin)*

1 lb. shrimp, shelled and deveined
Salt and pepper to taste
1 Tbsp. finely grated fresh ginger
1 tsp. cornstarch
½ cup good chicken stock
2 egg whites, barely beaten
3 Tbsps. chopped fresh chive
Soy sauce and finely chopped hot pepper to garnish

Salt and pepper shrimp, set aside. Dissolve cornstarch in a little stock, then stir in remaining stock and heat in a large frying pan, add shrimp and ginger. Cook stirring 3-4 minutes or till shrimp are cooked and stock slightly thickened. Add egg white in a slow stream, stirring constantly, when all the white has been added, remove from heat. Sprinkle with chives, stir, garnish with drops of soy sauce and hot pepper and serve immediately. SERVES 4.

TO PREPARE CONCHS - Knock a whole in the second joint from top of shell, insert a sharp knife and cut the muscle. Pull flesh out, pound with a wooden mallet to tenderize.

CONCH IMPERIAL

3 cups sliced pounded conch
3 Tbsps. butter
1 onion chopped fine or sliced
2 Tbsps flour
Chopped chive, thyme and a small piece of hot pepper
½ cup cream
Salt and black pepper to taste
2 Tbsps. each sherry and limejuice
¼ cup of mayonnaise
Heat butter, fry onions till soft, add flour, chives, thyme and hot pepper, stir to incorporate. Add cream, sherry, limejuice and mayonnaise, stir. Season with salt and pepper to taste. Add conch. Place in a greased casserole dish. Bake in a preheated 375F oven for 20 minutes. SERVES 6.

In days of 'Old' Sea Eggs or White Sea Urchins were sold in their shells topped with a seagrape leaf hat both filled to the brim with this gorgeous delicacy and at extremely reasonable prices. Alas! The plastic age has arrived and they are now sold by the "Bico" container at hugely exhorbitant prices.

SEA EGGS - FRIED OR STEAMED **(Serve over a bed of fluffy white rice or simply over a slice of buttered toast)**

3 sea egg cones or 1 "Bico" container
2 onions chopped fine
3 blades of chive minced
Small piece of hot pepper minced
Small piece sweet pepper minced
1 tsp. fresh thyme chopped
¼ cup butter
Salt and pepper to taste
Limejuice to taste

TO FRY: Heat butter in frying pan, add onions, chive, hot and sweet peppers, and the thyme, cook stirring 5-8 minutes. Add sea egg, salt, pepper and limejuice. Stir gently and cook 3-4 minutes.

TO STEAM: Combine all ingredients gently, place in a small meshed wire colander and steam over boiling water with a cover over the top for about 20 minutes. SERVES 6-8.

My father used to take a special gadget invented by him on picnics with us, he would dive up the sea egg, cut it open with his "toy", and simply dip the sea eggs into the sea and eat them. Simplicity itself and absolute fresh and gorgeous!

RAW SEA EGGS

Raw sea eggs
Limejuice
A bit of freshly grated black pepper
Sprinkle sea eggs with limejuice. Let sit for a few minutes, strain sprinkle with black pepper and serve. **Best eaten using your fingers.**

Conch Imperial

A true Caribbean delicacy - Sea Eggs or Sea Urchins as sold in days of old

Catch Of The Day

Barry's Fish. Gorgeous both baked or grilled on the BBQ

TO: BARRY, to whom this book is dedicated. I created this dish after talking to Barry, an orange vendor in Port-Of-Spain.
If you don't like the flavour of Chaddon Bene or cilantro, use parsley instead.

BARRY'S ORANGE FISH

2 fresh oranges
8 fish steaks or small whole Red Snappers, salt and pepper to taste
1 onion finely chopped
2 cloves garlic minced
2 Tbsps. chopped Trinidadian Chadon Bene or Cilantro, (Chinese Parsley)
Juice from ½ a lime
2 Tbsps. butter
1 tsp. sugar
Dash of Angostura bitters

Cut peel from 1 orange in a large continuous strips and reserve. Squeeze enough oranges to make ½ cup juice reserving remainder orange for use in garnishing. In a small saucepan melt the butter and fry the onion for 3 minutes but do not allow the butter nor onions to brown. Add the garlic and cook 2 minutes longer. Add orange juice, limejuice, sugar and bitters. Cool completely. Lightly salt and pepper fish steaks, place in a single layer in a baking pan and pour over the cooled orange mixture. Leave to marinate 1 hour at room temperature or longer in the refrigerator. Heat coals on a barbecue. Add reserved orange rind directly on to the coals. Grease barbecue grills, cook fish steaks turning once 4-5 minutes per side and whole fish 10-15 minutes per side, basting with reserved marinade. Fish may also be baked in the oven directly in a baking pan or casserole dish with all its marinade at 425F. for 20-25 minutes. Garnish with additional chopped cilantro and orange slices.
SERVES 4-6.

ESCOVITCH FISH *(Jamaican origin but similar recipes exist throughout the islands.)*
A simple grilled sweet potato - (see index) is a good accompaniment to this vinegary dish.

2½ lb. fish steaks
2 sweet peppers chopped
½ hot pepper minced
2 bay leaves
3 onions sliced
1 Tbsp. salt
2 garlic cloves minced
8 chives chopped
6 whole allspice bruised
Black pepper to taste
1 cup water
½ cup vinegar
¼ cup olive oil
Juice from 1-2 limes

Bring all ingredients except fish, oil, and limejuice to a boil. Cover, reduce heat and simmer 30 minutes. Meanwhile heat oil in a frying pan, fry fish till lightly browned, place fish in a deep casserole dish and pour over the hot vinegar mixture, season with lime juice and serve either hot or refrigerate and serve cold.
SERVES 8.

MARINADES FOR BARBECUE FISH
I have found that using a lot of oil in the marinade helps the fish from sticking to your grills. Oil the actual BBQ grills prior to cooking as well. Foil is often used to wrap BBQ fish. Try piercing a few skewer holes in the parcel to let the BBQ flavour penetrate.

FISH MARINADE 1
½ cup olive or corn oil
½ cup chopped onion
Juice from 1 lime
1 garlic clove minced
3 Tbsps. each chopped parsley and chives
Salt and pepper to taste.
Combine all ingredients in food processor or blender, blend till coarsely pureed. Pour over fish and marinate for 1 hour only. Lightly salt and pepper fish and barbecue or broil turning once
3-5 minutes per side.

This is excellent used with whole fish for the barbecue, stuff inner cavity with some of the butter mixture as well.

FISH MARINADE 2
¼ cup melted butter
3 Tbsps. each chopped fresh basil and parsley
2 garlic clove minced
Juice from 1 orange
Small piece hot pepper minced.
Salt and pepper to taste
Combine all ingredients, use to marinade and baste fish while broiling or barbecuing 3-5 minutes per side for steaks and 8-12 minutes per side for whole fish.

FISH MARINADE 3
¼ cup olive oil
Juice from 1 lime
½ cup chadon bene or cilantro chopped fine
¼ cup fresh minced parsley
¼ cup grated onion
1 Tbsp. sugar
Small piece of hot pepper minced
Salt and pepper to taste
Whisk all ingredients together. Marinate fish 2 hours in refrigerator. Broil or barbecue
3-5 minutes per side.

PAN SEARED/GRILLED FISH STEAKS *(Cajun Seasoning resembles our creole spices)*
4 fish steaks
Prepared Cajun Seasoning- generous amount
1 Tbsp. each minced parley, chive, thyme and onion
½ Tbsp. each melted butter and olive oil combined
Orange or Lime slice to garnish
Sprinkle fish with Cajun seasoning, parsley, chive, thyme and onion. Baste with butter and oil mixture on both sides. Pan fry or grill 3-4 minutes per side. Garnish with lime or orange slice.
SERVES 4.

Barbecuing fish on a coal pot

Pan Seared or Grilled fish steaks

Catch Of The Day

Carol frying Flying Fish at THE COVE restaurant

FRIED FISH

METHOD 1

Salt and pepper to taste
Seasoning - *see SEASONING in index*
Flour to dredge
2 eggs beaten with a little milk
Soft fresh breadcrumbs
Oil for shallow frying
Make slits in fish and stuff with seasoning, salt and pepper both sides, dip in flour, then egg and quote with crumbs. Place on a cookie sheet and let rest 15 minutes. Heat oil and fry turning once till cooked and golden.

METHOD 2

As above but use half dry breadcrumbs and half cornmeal for final coating.

METHOD 3

As above but make a thin batter with the egg, a ¼ cup of flour and a pinch of baking powder. Dip the fish directly into the batter then in dry breadcrumbs and fry.

FRIED BAJAN FLYING FISH

10 prepared or deboned flying fish
Lime and water
4 Tbsps. Bajan Seasoning - *see SEASONING in index*
Salt and pepper to taste
Flour mixed with a little powdered clove for dredging
2 eggs beaten with a little milk
Dry breadcrumbs to quote
Oil for shallow frying
Soak fish in lime and water no more than 10 minutes, pat dry. Salt and pepper fish, equally distribute seasoning between grooves of fish. Coat fish with seasoned flour, then with egg mixture and finally with crumbs. Rest for 15 minutes. Fry in oil till just golden. SERVES 5.

No relative of Flipper. Better known as Dorado or Mahi Mahi fish. One of the most moist and delicious fish that comes from our waters, like all fish, do not overcook or the fish becomes hard and chewy.

DOLPHIN-BATTER FRIED

8 dolphin steaks
Salt and pepper to taste
6 Tbsps. seasoning - *see recipe in index*
1 Tbsp. hot pepper sauce
1 cup flour
1 heaping tsp. baking powder
¾ - 1cup water
1 Tbsp. oil
Mix seasoning, pepper sauce, flour, baking powder, water and oil till lump free. Lightly salt and pepper fish, dust with flour, dip in batter and deep fat fry. Serve with hot sauce. SERVES 4.

CARIBBEAN BAKED STUFFED RED SNAPPER.

STUFFING: ¾ - 1 cup fresh breadcrumbs depending on size of fish cavity

   ¼ cup melted butter

   2 chopped chives

   2 Tbsps. chopped parsley

   Small piece of hot pepper minced

   1 onion grated

   Juice from 1 lime

   2 tsps. fresh chopped thyme

   Salt and pepper to taste

Mix all above ingredients well in a mixing bowl.

1 SNAPPER: cleaned, scaled, deboned with head and tail left on about 4 lbs.

   Salt and pepper to taste

   ¼ cup butter melted with a small garlic clove and a little limejuice

Lightly brush inside of snapper with some butter, garlic and limejuice mixture. Place stuffing in cavity and secure with skewers or toothpicks. Baste both sides of fish with some of the butter garlic mixture, salt and pepper both sides and bake in a hot 475F. Oven for 20 minutes. Just before serving pour remaining butter mixture over fish or warm and serve in a separate bowl. SERVES 4.

PINEAPPLE CHINESE FISH

2 lbs. fish cut in 1" cubes

1 tsp. each salt and grated fresh ginger

2 Tbsps. each dry sherry and cornflour or cornstarch

1 egg white, lightly beaten

1x 10 oz. can pineapple chunks, drained, reserving liquid.

2 Tbsps. soy sauce

1½ tsps. sugar

½ cup oil

¼ of a hot pepper chopped

Chives to garnish

Mix salt, ginger, sherry, 1Tbsp. of the cornflour and egg white then rub it into the fish. Marinate 25 minutes. In separate bowl combine remaining cornflour with reserved pineapple juice, soy sauce and sugar. Heat oil in a frying pan, add hot pepper and fry one minute. Add fish and fry turning carefully for 1 minute per side. Remove fish, set aside and remove all but 2Tbsps. oil from pan. Add pineapple to pan and fry for three minutes; add juice mixture and cook stirring till slightly thickened, return fish and juices to pan and cook 2-3 minutes longer. Garnish with chopped chives. SERVES 6.

DOLPHIN-BAKED IN LIME SAUCE

8 dolphin steaks

Salt and pepper to taste

1 recipe white sauce - **_see recipe in index_**

Juice from 1-2 limes

Buttered breadcrumbs

¼ cup chopped fresh chives

¼ cup chopped parsley

Salt and pepper fish steaks and place in a buttered casserole dish in a single layer. Add limejuice and chives to white sauce, pour over fish, dot with breadcrumbs and bake in a preheated 475F. oven for 20 minutes. SERVES 4.

Caribbean Baked stuffed Snapper

Pineapple Chinese Fish

Catch Of The Day

Coconut Fish

COCONUT FISH

1 lb. fish cut in 3" pieces
1 garlic clove minced
Salt and pepper to taste
Juice from 1 lime
1 tsp. fresh thyme chopped
Dried ginger
3 Tbsps. butter
2 onions sliced thin
1 Tbsp. flour
1 cup coconut milk
2 Tbsps. parsley
Small piece hot pepper
Season fish with garlic, salt and pepper, limejuice, thyme and some dried ginger, set-aside for 30 minutes. Heat butter and fry fish till just golden 2-3 minutes, set aside. In same saucepan, fry onions till golden, add flour and cook stirring till dissolved. Add coconut milk slowly, stirring constantly till mixture is smooth. Add parsley and hot pepper, return fish to pan and cook covered over low heat for 10 minutes. SERVES 4.

SNAPPER AND CALLALOO *(My brother-in-law's favourite, particularly when I serve it with red sweet pepper sauce. This fish dish has become a ritual for me to cook on my Birthday with Janette always managing to locate a fresh snapper for me)*

1 whole snapper 3-4 lbs. scaled, gutted, cleaned and deboned-head left on
Salt and pepper to taste
Juice from 1-2 limes
6 Tbsps. butter
1 bunch callaloo or spinach leaves chopped
1 onion minced
1 garlic clove minced
¼ red hot pepper minced
¼ tsp. grated nutmeg
½ cup fresh breadcrumbs
White wine
Sprinkle limejuice and lightly salt and pepper both cavity and outside of fish. Set aside. In small saucepan melt 4 Tbsps. of the butter and fry the onion, garlic and hot pepper 3-4 minutes, add callaloo and nutmeg and cook stirring till tender. Add breadcrumbs, salt and pepper mixture to taste and cool completely. Stuff cavity with callaloo mixture, secure with toothpicks or skewers. Place fish in a well buttered baking pan. Dot with the remaining butter, drizzle top with a little white wine and bake in a preheated 425F. Oven 20-30 minutes depending on size. Serve with red pepper sauce - *recipe follows*.
SERVES 4.

RED SWEET PEPPER SAUCE

Sautee 2 red sweet peppers coarsely chopped, 1 onion finely chopped, 1 garlic clove minced in ¼ cup butter for 10 minutes over low heat. Add ½ cup sherry, 1 chicken stock cube and ¼ cup water. Cook 5 minutes more over medium heat. Roughly blend mixture in blender, leaving some vegetable chunks. Return to pan and add ½ cup cream, 4 Tbsps. chopped basil, a dash of Tobasco pepper sauce and salt and pepper to taste. Rewarm before serving.

A Jamaican dish traditionally served with boiled green bananas.

MACKEREL RUN DOWN or DIP AND FALL BACK

2 lbs. salted mackerel, soaked in water to cover for at least 6 hours and deboned.
5 cups coconut milk
1 garlic clove minced
2 large onions chopped fine
4 blades chive chopped
2 sprigs fresh thyme chopped
2 tomatoes cut in chunks
2 Tbsps. tomato ketchup
1 whole hot pepper
Dash of ground allspice
Dash of fresh limejuice
Bring coconut milk to a boil, reduce heat and simmer adding the garlic, onions, chives, thyme, tomatoes, ketchup and whole hot pepper. Simmer till custard like mixture forms, about 20 minutes. Add fish, allspice and lime juice. Cook a further 10-15 minutes. Serve with boiled peeled green bananas.
SERVES 4-6.

FISH CURRY

6 fish steaks
Salt and pepper to taste
2 Tbsps. oil
2 onions chopped
1 heaping Tbsp. curry powder
1 garlic clove minced
1 tomato chopped
Small piece hot pepper minced
1 cup coconut milk
Juice of ½ a lime
Salt and pepper fish, set aside. Heat oil in large frying pan, cook onions over low heat 5 minutes, add curry powder and garlic, cook 3 minutes, add tomato and hot pepper and cook a further minute or so. Add coconut milk and cook about 10 minutes or till mixture thickens, add fish and continue cooking turning once till fish tests done, 5-8 minutes. Sprinkle with limejuice.
SERVES 4.

JERKED FISH

8 fish steaks
Salt to taste
4 Tbsps. 'jerk seasoning'- *see recipe in index*
¼ cup olive oil
Combine jerk seasoning and oil, rub all over fish and leave to marinate 2-3 hours in the fridge. Lightly salt the fish steaks, grill or barbecue turning once for 3-5 minutes per side. SERVES 4-6.

SEVICHE FISH

Use raw fish such as tuna, bonito or kingfish cut into small cubes. Marinate in ¼ cup limejuice for 1-2 hours. Strain, rinse lightly, mix with salt, hot pepper, chopped onion, chive, sweet pepper, tomatoes, olive oil and parsley. Season to taste with fresh limejuice. CHILL.

Makerel Run Down or Dip and Fall Back - named as the sauce runs down or falls back into your plate

Seviche fish

Fried Shark for Shark & Bake with Chadon Bene sauce - Sold by street vendors all over Trinidad

BOILED FISH

2 fish steaks, salt and pepper to taste
1 Tbsp.each limejuice and "seasoning" *see recipe in index*
3 Tbsps. butter
1 garlic clove minced
2 onions sliced
2 tomatoes sliced
Chopped fresh parsley to garnish
Salt and pepper fish, sprinkle with limejuice, make slits into fish and stuff with seasoning. Set aside to rest for 1 hour. Heat butter in a saucepan, add garlic and onions, fry 2-3 minutes, add tomatoes, cover, and cook till slightly thickened about 5-8 minutes. Add fish and any remaining marinade, cover and simmer 8-10 minutes. Garnish with chopped parsley.
SERVES 2.

FRIED SHARK - FOR SHARK & BAKE *(a Trinidadian Dish served in bakes with chadon bene sauce- see recipe in index)*

1 lb. young shark, cut into steaks
Flour seasoned with salt and lots of black pepper
2 Tbsps. each minced fresh thyme and chives
1 tsp. minced garlic
½ tsp. hot pepper sauce
Limejuice and salt
Soak shark in limejuice and salt for 5 minutes. Drain, rub steaks with thyme, chives, garlic and pepper sauce. Dredge in seasoned flour and deep fat fry. Drain on kitchen paper. Serve in a cut bake with chadon bene sauce - *see index for both recipes.*
SERVES 4.

MUM'S FISH SALAD *(I love leftovers over hot buttered toast for breakfast)*

4 cups cooked flaked fresh fish
1 cup mayonnaise, preferably homemade - *recipe follows*
1 lb. freshly cooked asparagus or tinned, drained thoroughly
1 cup frozen green peas, boiled in salted water for 3 minutes and cooled
Olives for garnish
Layer 2 cups fish in casserole dish, top with half the asparagus, half the green peas and half the mayonnaise, sprinkle with freshly ground black pepper and salt to taste. Repeat layers. Garnish with sliced olives. Chill 2-3 hours.
SERVES 6.

Home made mayonnaise must be refrigerated, use within 2 days.

MAYONNAISE FOR FISH

2 whole eggs
⅔ cup olive oil
1 tsp. each dry mustard powder and salt
2 tsps. sugar
4 Tbsps. fresh limejuice
1⅓ cups corn oil
Place all ingredients except the corn oil in a food processor. Process 8 seconds. Slowly add corn oil through shute. Process 10 seconds longer once all of the oil has been added. Thin if necessary with a little fish stock. MAKES ABOUT 2 CUPS.

FISH CREAM

2 cups cooked flaked fish
Salt and pepper to taste
2 Tbsps. butter
1 small onion chopped
2 blades chive chopped
4 Tbsps. chopped fresh parsley
2 Tbsps. flour
1½ cups evaporated milk
Juice from ½ a lime
1 cup grated cheddar cheese
2 Tbsps, sherry

Melt butter in saucepan, add onion, chive and parsley, cook 2-3 minutes. Add flour, cook 1 minute, slowly add milk whisking continuously. Cook stirring till thickened, season with salt, pepper and limejuice, add half the cheese, the sherry and the fish. Pour into a greased casserole or individual ramekin dishes, top with remaining cheese and bake in a preheated 375F. Oven for 20 minutes.
SERVES 4.

Frizzled salt fish is served over scrambled eggs for breakfast or over rice as a main meal.

FRIZZLED SALT FISH

½ lb. salt fish, soaked in water to cover overnight - bones removed
1 onion chopped fine
3 chives chopped
2 sprigs fresh thyme chopped
5 Tbsps. oil
Small piece hot pepper minced
Chopped fresh parsley for garnish

Flake fish very finely - preferably pound the fish in a mortar and pestle, combine with remaining ingredients. Heat oil in a heavy frying pan, add salt fish and fry over high heat till golden and crispy. Sprinkle with chopped parsley before serving. SERVES 4.

Stuffed breadfruit is a rather dry dish, serve with lots of additional butter or make additional filling adding water or stock to make good gravy to serve alongside.

BAKED SALT FISH STUFFED BREADFRUIT

8 ozs. salt fish soaked in water to cover overnight - deboned
6 Tbsps. butter
2 each large onions and tomatoes chopped
1 sweet pepper chopped
½ a small hot pepper minced
1 garlic clove minced
Minced fresh thyme and marjoram to taste.

Melt butter, fry onion, tomato, sweet and hot pepper, garlic, thyme and marjoram. Cook 5 minutes. Add 2 cups water, cook 10 minutes. Add flaked salt fish and adjust seasoning with salt and pepper to taste. Cool.
TO PREPARE STUFFED BREADFRUIT: Wash breadfruit leaving skin on. Carefully cut a large round out of top of breadfruit and remove core, keeping top of breadfruit intact. Stuff with filling, reserving the liquid to use as gravy. Replace top and nail together by using skewers. Place directly on hot coals and cook turning often for about 30-40 minutes, or place in a baking pan and bake at 375.F. for 1½ hours or till breadfruit is tender. Serve with reserved gravy.
SERVES 6.

Catch Of The Day

Two scenes from Grenada

The Black "Buck" Pots

Village life - BARBADOS

108

The Black "Buck" Pots

A selection of my black "buck" pots, some inherited, some carefully 'seasoned' through the years

Our "Hot Pots" or main meat dishes may consist of stews-a true Caribbean medley, barbecuing jerked meats-an art born out of Jamaica, roasting beef and lamb with that aromatic scent wafting through your home on a Sunday morning, frying our wonderfully seasoned poultry, baking stuffed pork or chicken with our array of herbed stuffings. Preparing this part of your meal is perhaps the most important for it is the end result of careful cooking that will flavor the accompaniments to your meal.

One thing I can truly say is that we in the Caribbean like a lot of good gravies and sauces and certainly in large quantities to accompany our rice (traditional with almost every meal) and our 'Provisions'.

Please use these recipes as a guidance for in each person and island our taste buds vary. If you like more garlic, or more onion or better still more hot peppers...simply add more to suit your tastes! For I shall repeat again the importance of making this part of your meal the piece de resistance!

Lamb is eaten through out the islands but strangely goat is eaten almost everywhere except Barbados, perhaps it is because Barbados produces a black belly sheep which is unique to her - A flavour I would describe as a slightly gamey version of lamb.

I once read that a phenomenon with all islands through out the world is the volume of pork consumed, we in the Caribbean are no exception to this rule and our pork is some of the best to be found anywhere.

Duck breasts with mango

CREOLE SALMI OF DUCK *(Chicken or rabbit can be substituted)*

1 duck cut in serving pieces
½ cup orange juice
2 Tbsps. Angostura bitters
Salt and pepper to taste
½ cup dry sherry
2 large onions chopped
3 cloves garlic minced
4 chives chopped
2 Tbsps. fresh thyme
½ small hot pepper minced
3 Tbsps. oil
6 Tbsps. brown sugar
¼ cup pimento stuffed olives
¼ cup orange liqueur

Marinate the duck with the orange juice, bitters, salt and pepper, sherry, onions, garlic, chives, thyme and hot pepper overnight in the fridge. Heat oil in a heavy saucepan, add sugar and cook 3-4 minutes or till mixture caramelizes, carefully fry the duck pieces in batches turning to brown. Return the duck with its marinade to the pot, cover, bring to a boil, reduce heat and simmer for 1 hour. Remove cover, add olives and boil till mixture thickens slightly. Pour liqueur over and serve. SERVES 4.

MULATTO DUCK *(Substitute chicken or rabbit if desired)*

1 duck
3 garlic cloves minced
Juice from 2 limes
1 small hot pepper minced
6 whole cloves
2 cups chicken stock
¼ cup oil
1 cup fresh orange juice
Salt and pepper to taste.

Rub duck inside and out with the garlic, limejuice and hot pepper. Sprinkle with salt and pepper and refrigerate 4 hours or overnight. Heat oil in a large frying pan. Brown duck all over and place in casserole dish. Pour in the stock and orange juice, add the cloves and bake covered in a 350F. Oven for 1 hour. Remove cover, baste with the pan juices and continue to bake uncovered for 45 minutes more. Garnish with orange slices if liked. SERVES 4.

DUCK BREASTS WITH MANGO *(replace with chicken breast for a change)*

2 boneless duck breasts pounded between sheets of waxed paper
Salt and pepper to taste
Ground cardamom seeds
Mango slices
3 Tbsps. butter melted
1 Tbsp. Caribbean brown sugar

Salt and pepper duck breasts. Broil 5-8 minutes per side starting with skin side up. Return to skin side up, place mango slices over breasts and sprinkle with cardamom, brush all over with melted butter and sprinkle tops with the sugar. Broil 2-3 minutes more. SERVES 2.

ROASTED - STUFFED CHICKEN

1 whole chicken
Salt and pepper to taste
Paprika to taste
6 slices bacon diced
¼ cup butter
2 onions chopped
2 stalks of celery chopped
Liver and gizzard from chicken, cut into small chunks
2 garlic cloves minced
¼ cup chopped chives
Small piece hot pepper minced
1 Tbsp. fresh chopped thyme
½ cup seedless raisins
6 olives sliced
1 Tbsp. Worcestershire sauce
2 cups breadcrumbs or crushed crackers or cubed bread
¼ cup stock or water to bind
Additional salt and pepper to taste
Prepare stuffing: Cook bacon and butter till bacon softens and fat is rendered, add onions, celery, liver and gizzard and cook till no longer pink about 5 minutes. Add garlic, chives, hot pepper, thyme and cook for a further 3-4 minutes. Remove from heat and stir in raisins, olives, Worcestershire, breadcrumbs and stock. Salt and pepper to taste. Cool. Stuff chicken, close opening with skewers, sprinkle chicken all over with paprika, salt and pepper, place in a baking pan and bake in a preheated 325F. Oven for 1½ hours. SERVES 6.

CHICKEN CURRIED *(use to fill Rotis or serve with plain boiled rice. Also excellent accompanied by separate small dishes of chopped onion, chopped pineapple, chutney, grated coconut, sliced bananas, chopped tomatoes, chopped nuts, grated cucumber etc)*

1 chicken cut in joints
Salt and pepper to taste
2 Tbsps. oil
2 large onions chopped
3 garlic cloves minced
1 tsp. saffron powder or turmeric
1 tsp. cumin or geera seed
3 Tbsps. curry powder
Small piece hot pepper
1" piece of fresh ginger grated
Salt and pepper chicken. Heat oil in a large heavy saucepan, fry onions 2-3 minutes, add garlic, saffron powder, cumin, curry powder, hot pepper and ginger, fry for a further 2-3 minutes. Add chicken parts and stir till coated with the curry mixture. Cover pot tightly, bring to a boil, reduce heat and simmer 35-40 minutes. *A little water may be added but if simmered gently a good stock results from the cooking process.*

TO MAKE CHICKEN AND POTATO FILLING FOR ROTIS - remove chicken meat from bones, set aside. Add peeled cubed potatoes to liquid, cover pot and cook till potatoes are tender. Return meat and reheat SERVES 4-6.

The Black "Buck" Pots

A Sunday roasted Stuffed Chicken

Curried chicken

Chicken Fried: Consumed in mass amounts through out the Caribbean, shown with Macaroni pie

The Black "Buck" Pots

CHICKEN FRIED

1 chicken cut in joints
Juice of 1 fresh lime
Salt and pepper to taste
2-3 Tbsps. "BAJAN SEASONING" - *see index*
1 Tbsp. "BAJAN" Hot sauce - *see index*
1 egg beaten with ¼ cup milk
Flour to coat
Oil for deep fat frying
Make gashes in each piece of chicken and stuff with some of the seasoning. Rub joints with limejuice, salt, pepper, Bajan seasoning, hot sauce and egg mixture, leave to season for at least ½ an hour or preferably overnight in fridge. Place flour in a plastic bag, add chicken two pieces at a time, shake till coated and arrange on a rack. Let rest for 10 minutes. Fry chicken in batches in hot oil 15-20 minutes total time. SERVES 4.

TROPICAL CHICKEN

1 chicken cut up, salt and pepper to taste
1 cup of any BBQ sauce
8 oz. can crushed pineapple well drained
1 Tbsp. Tabasco sauce
Preheat oven to 350F. Reserve about 4 tablespoons of the pineapple. Combine remaining pineapple with the BBQ sauce and Tabasco sauce. Lightly salt and pepper chicken and place in single layer skin side up in large baking pan. Pour over the BBQ mixture and bake covered for 30 minutes. Remove cover, dot with the reserved pineapple and continue baking uncovered for 20-30 minutes longer or till cooked. SERVES 4.

CHICKEN STEW *(Creole style - add dumplings if liked - see index)*

1 chicken jointed, salt and pepper to taste
2 large onions chopped
4 sprigs chives, chopped
3 cloves garlic minced
2 tsps. fresh chopped thyme
1 tsp. fresh chopped marjoram
Small piece of hot pepper minced
2 Tbsps. Worcestershire sauce
1 Tbsp. Angostura bitters
4 carrots sliced
3 potatoes diced (optional)
2 Tbsps. oil
¼ cup sugar
Season chicken with salt, pepper, onions, chives, garlic, thyme, marjoram, hot pepper, Worcestershire and bitters. Leave to marinate 2 hours or overnight in fridge. Heat oil in a large heavy saucepan, add sugar and cook till mixture turns a deep brown colour, watch carefully as you do not want mixture to burn, carefully cook chicken in caramel in batches. Return chicken to the pan, add all of the marinade, cook 5 minutes. Add 1 cup water or chicken stock, the carrots, bring to a boil, cover with a tight fitting lid, reduce heat to low and simmer chicken 40 minutes. If potatoes are to be added, add 20 minutes before end of cooking time. SERVES 6.

The Black "Buck" Pots

ORANGE CHICKEN

1 chicken cut into pieces, salt and pepper to taste
2 tsps. curry powder
Grated rind of 1 orange
¼ cup fresh orange juice
2 Tbsps. honey
1 Tbsp. prepared mustard
Orange slices for garnish

Salt and pepper chicken pieces, sprinkle both sides with the curry powder rubbing in the mixture well. Place in a baking pan, skin side up. Combine remaining ingredients and pour over the chicken. Bake in a preheated 375F oven for 1 hour, basting with any accumulated juices. Remove chicken from pan onto a platter, garnish with orange slices. Make a sauce if wanted by dissolving 2 tsps. cornstarch in 4 Tbsps. water, add to chicken pan with 2 Tbsps. marmalade, 2 Tbsps. each orange liqueur and brandy. Cook stirring in brown bits at bottom of pan till slightly thickened. SERVES 6.

CURRY GLAZED CHICKEN WINGS

24 chicken wings, salt and pepper to taste
¼ cup honey
¼ cup soy sauce
2 Tbsps. grated fresh ginger
2 garlic cloves minced
1 Tbsp. curry powder

Combine honey, soy sauce, ginger, garlic and curry powder. Lightly salt and pepper wings to taste, pour over honey mixture turning to coat all sides and leave to marinate for 2 hours or overnight in refrigerator. Place in greased baking pan in a single layer, pour over any remaining marinade and bake in a preheated 400F. Oven for 30-35 minutes. SERVES 6.

CHICKEN STUFFED WITH CALLALOO or SPINACH

4 chicken breast halves, salt and pepper to taste.
8 whole callaloo leaves or spinach
1 tsp. dried mustard
1 cup grated mozzarella cheese

Place callaloo leaves in salted boiling water to soften for 3 minutes, remove from water and cool. Pound chicken between sheets of waxed paper, salt and pepper skinless side. Sprinkle with dried mustard, place 2 callaloo leaves on this side, top with the cheese and completely enclose the cheese with the leaves. Roll up the chicken like a cigar, secure with string, skewers or toothpicks. Lightly salt and pepper skin side and bake in a preheated 400F. Oven for 20-25 minutes or till chicken is cooked. SERVES 4.

CHICKEN JERKED *(Jamaican origin)*

1 chicken cut into joints
¼ cup corn or olive oil
¼ cup prepared jerk seasoning - s*ee recipe in index*
Salt to taste

Mix oil and jerk seasoning, rub all over chicken joints, salt to taste and leave to marinate for 30 minutes or preferably overnight. Cook chicken on grill or barbecue turning every 10 minutes for approximately 30 minutes or till cooked. SERVES 4.

116

Curry glazed Chicken wings

Chicken stuffed with callaloo

Lime grilled chicken

CHICKEN in GINGER SAUCE *(Caribbean Chinese origin)*

1 whole chicken

4 cups water

4" piece of fresh ginger crushed

2 tsps. sesame oil

2 Tbsps. corn oil

1 cup chopped chives

2" piece of fresh ginger, peeled, cut in thin strips

4 tsps. soy sauce or more to taste

Salt and pepper to taste

Bring water to a boil in a large pot, add crushed ginger and chicken, bring back to a boil, lower heat and simmer chicken for 35-40 minutes or till cooked. Cool completely in liquid. Cut meat into serving sized portions. Meanwhile heat both oils in a frying pan, add chives and ginger, stir fry a minute or so, remove from heat, add soy sauce and pour over chicken, salt and pepper to taste and serve. immediately. SERVES 4.

My daughters favourite way with wings
CHICKEN WINGS

16 chicken wings, salt and pepper to taste

¼ cup pepper jelly - *see recipe index*

¼ cup ketchup

1tsp. Worcestershire sauce

Salt and pepper chicken wings, set aside. Heat remaining ingredients in a small saucepan till jelly dissolves. Grill or barbecue wings 5 minutes per side. Baste with sauce and continue cooking, basting and turning frequently for a further 20 minutes or till wings are cooked through. SERVES 4.

I often use this recipe when cooked chicken is required for other dishes. It is delicious in its simplicity and by thickening the liquid with a little cornstarch and water or cream is excellent served over pasta topped with grilled Caribbean vegetables.
SIMPLY STEEPED CHICKEN BREAST

2 boneless chicken breasts, salt and pepper to taste

2-4 Tbsps. fresh chopped basil

¼ cup each white wine and water

Salt and pepper chicken breasts, sprinkle tops with basil. Bring water and wine to a boil, lower heat, add chicken, cover and barely simmer 5-8 minutes. Turn off heat and leave covered to steep in the stock and cool. SERVES 2.

LIME GRILLED CHICKEN

1 chicken quartered, salt and pepper to taste

⅓ cup fresh limejuice

½ cup melted butter

1 tsp. fresh thyme

¼ tsp. West Indian Hot Sauce

¼ cup brown sugar

Combine limejuice, butter, thyme, hot sauce and sugar. Salt and pepper chicken to taste. Oil a BBQ or broiler grid, cook basting chicken with lime sauce for 30-40 minutes turning and basting often. SERVES 4.

The Black "Buck" Pots

BOILED CHICKEN FOR SALADS

1 whole chicken, salt and pepper to taste.
2 tsps. fresh thyme
1 stalk celery
1 onion sliced

Salt and pepper chicken, place in a saucepan with the thyme, celery and onion. Pour over 1 cup of water, bring to a boil, lower heat, cover and simmer 40 minutes. Turn off heat and leave to cool in the stock. RESERVE STOCK FOR USE IN SOUPS, PIES OR CASSEROLLES. When cool, refrigerate till chicken is cold as it is easier to handle. Remove skin and bones and cut into meat into small pieces. SERVES 6.

CHICKEN AND VEGETABLE SALAD

Combine the following and mix into the above chicken pieces:
½ cup mayonnaise, ½ cup crisp cooked diced carrots, ½ cup crisp cooked green peas, ½ cup chopped celery, 1 onion chopped, juice from ½ a lime, 1 Tbsp. prepared mustard and salt and pepper to taste. SERVES 6.

SWEET CURRY SALAD

Combine the following and mix into chicken pieces:
½ cup mayonnaise, 1 Tbsp. curry powder, 1 onion chopped, 2 Tbsps. mango chutney chopped. SERVES 6.

HERBED SALAD

Combine the following and mix into chicken pieces:
½ cup mayonnaise, ¼ cup each chopped chives and parsley, 1 onion chopped, 1 sweet pepper chopped. SERVES 6.

We grew up with this chicken pie. Sometimes Mum would prepare it with cooked jointed chicken pieces, bone and all. To a West Indian there is nothing sweeter than picking up a bone and chewing away.
CHICKEN PIE

Melt 3 Tbsps. butter in a saucepan, add 3 Tbsps. flour stirring, add 1½ cups RESERVED chicken stock, cook stirring till thickened. Add 2 Tbsps. sherry. Combine sauce with cooked cubed carrots, green peas, onion, canned sliced mushrooms and celery. Place in pie dish, add a pastry topping of your choice and bake according to pastry directions.
OR: BISCUIT TOPPING - Combine 2 cups flour with 2 tsps. baking powder, 1 tsp. salt. Mix in ½ cup shortening till mixture resembles fine crumbs. Add ⅓ cup water combined with 1 beaten egg. Roll out to ¼" thick and top pie. Bake 375F preheated oven for 25-30 minutes. SERVES 6.

CHICKEN CASSEROLE # 1

Place chicken mixture with vegetables and sauce as above in a pie plate. Top with buttered crumbs. Sprinkle with paprika and bake as above. SERVES 6.

CHICKEN CASSEROLE # 2

Place chicken mixture with vegetables and sauce as above in a pie plate. Top with cooked peeled sweet potatoes or yam that have been mashed with milk, butter, salt and pepper. Drizzle top with melted butter and bake as above. SERVES 6.

Chicken salad and Mum's Chicken pie

Rum Glazed Ham for festive occasions

The Black "Buck" Pots

HOLIDAY TURKEY

10-12 lb. Turkey - reserve giblets
Salt, pepper and paprika to taste
½ cup melted butter plus additional for basting
½ cup diced dried apricots
½ cup raisins
½ cup Caribbean rum
½ cup butter
2 onions chopped
2 apples cored and chopped
2 tsps. fresh thyme
1 tsp. dried sage
2 tsps. curry powder
¼ cup each chopped fresh parsley and chives
½ loaf of white sliced bread cut into ¼"cubes
1 cup water or chicken stock
Salt and pepper to taste

PREPARE STUFFING: Chop giblets into small pieces. Soak apricots and raisins in rum for 10 minutes. Melt butter in large saucepan, fry giblets till cooked, add onions, apples, thyme, sage, curry powder, parsley and chives. Cook 10 minutes till onions are soft. Add fruit and rum mixture. Fold in bread cubes and moisten with water or stock. Salt and pepper to taste. Cool completely.

TO COOK TURKEY: Preheat oven to 325F. Stuff turkey with cooled stuffing. Sew or skewer opening closed. Sprinkle with salt, pepper and paprika, place on a rack in a roasting pan to fit the turkey. Bake for 1 hour. Baste turkey with melted butter, bake 1 hour longer. Increase heat to 375F, baste turkey again with butter and cook 40-50 minutes longer. Insert meat thermometer in thigh and cook till thermometer shows required temperature for turkey basting every 10 minutes towards end of cooking. SERVES 10-14.

TO MAKE GRAVY: Remove turkey from roasting pan, set aside. To juices in the pan add ¼ cup flour and cook stirring till incorporated. Slowly add chicken stock or water and cook whisking constantly till slightly thickened. Add a chicken stock cube if required for a more intense flavour but taste first to check on saltiness.

HAM

8-10 lbs. bone in precooked Ham
20-30 whole cloves
Pineapple rings, Maraschino cherries cut in half or sliced oranges for garnish
HAM GLAZE 1: 2 Tbsps. melted butter, ½ cup Caribbean brown sugar
                2 Tbsps. prepared mustard, ¼ cup rum
HAM GLAZE 2: 2 Tbsps. melted butter, ¼ cup brown sugar
                ¼ cup orange marmalade, 2 Tbsps. orange liqueur
Combine one of the above glaze ingredients in a small saucepan, cook over medium heat till sugar is dissolved. Set aside to cool. Remove skin from ham, score fat into diamond shapes, insert a whole clove in each diamond. Place in a roasting pan and cook in a preheated 350F. Oven for 35 minutes. Baste with some of the glaze and return to oven for a further 35minutes, basting with glaze every 10 minutes. Place pineapple rings with halved cherries in the center of pineapple, or orange slices accordingly. Secure with toothpicks, glaze fruit and cook 10 minutes more.
SERVES 10-14

Usually peas and rice accompany this roast, this is my husbands favourite Sunday meal. Other accompaniments are roasted sweet potatoes and a creamed cheesey white sauced vegetable.

BAKED PORK

1 leg of pork, about 10 lbs.

Juice from 2 limes

2-3 Tbsps. "seasoning"- *see recipe in index*

1 Tbsp. salt

Black pepper to taste

Score skin in diamond shapes as you would a ham. Pierce pork through flesh at various intervals and stuff with "seasoning". Rub limejuice all over and then pat the salt on. Pepper to taste. The pork may be refrigerated overnight to marinate or may be baked right away. Preheat oven to 375F. Bake pork covered with foil for 2 hours. Increase oven temperature to 475F. Remove foil. Brush skin with oil from pan sprinkle the skin with additional salt. Bake 20-30 minutes longer or till skin crisps up.

TO MAKE PAN GRAVY: slice 1 onion finely, fry in the pan juices 2-3 minutes, add 4 Tbsps. flour and stir, mixing to incorporate. Add 3 cups water or chicken stock slowly and cook stirring continuously. Lower heat and simmer gently 10-15 minutes. If more flavour is required add a tablespoon of "seasoning" and continue simmering.

SERVES 8-10.

When I am feeling lazy, I simply cook these in a roasting pan in the oven.

JERKED PORK CHOPS

8 pork chops

Salt to taste

4 Tbsps. jerk "seasoning"- *see recipe in index*

¼ cup oil

Make gashes throughout pork chops and stuff with seasoning, combine remaining seasoning with the oil and pour all over both sides of pork. Salt pork and allow to rest a couple of hours or preferably overnight in the refrigerator. (Better still for 48 hours in the refrigerator) Barbecue or grill chops turning frequently till cooked through.

Jerk seasoning varies in the amount of Pepper Heat! Because of this I like to accompany this meal with some grilled sweet potatoes - (see recipe in index) and a good sweetish fritter such as pumpkin.

SERVES 4.

Traditionally seasoned with Caribbean seasonings but any prepared seasoning will do

BREADED PORK CHOPS

8 thin pork chops

Juice from 1 lime

2 Tbsps. "seasoning"- *see recipe in index*

Salt and pepper to taste

½ cup flour

2 eggs beaten with a little milk

1 cup dry breadcrumbs

Rub pork chops with limejuice, seasoning and salt and pepper, let rest for a few hours. Pat some of the seasoning on each chop before dipping in flour, then eggs then crumbs. Fry in oil till browned, crisp and cooked through.

SERVES 4.

Jerked pork chops

Breaded pork chops

Pork & Red beans, real soul food

The Black "Buck" Pots

PORK AND RED BEANS

1 lb. pork stew
1 salted pigtail, soaked overnight then cut in pieces
1 clove garlic minced
1 onion chopped
Small piece hot pepper minced
1 tsp. sugar
2 cups dried red beans, soaked overnight in water to cover
1 cup coconut milk
Salt and pepper to taste
3 Tbsps. Oil
Heat oil in a large saucepan, add pork and brown, add garlic, onion and hot pepper cook 2-3 minutes, add pigtail and rinsed beans. Add coconut milk and enough water to cover beans. Bring to a boil, lower heat and simmer for 1-1½ hours or till beans are soft, adding additional water to barely cover beans as necessary but mixture should be fairly thick for serving. Salt and pepper to taste.
SERVES 4.

HONEYED PORK CHOPS

4 pork chops
Garlic powder to taste
Salt and pepper to taste
¼ cup each honey and soy sauce
2 tsps. freshly grated ginger
1 tsp. prepared mustard
Combine all ingredients except pork chops. Place pork chops in a single layer in a dish, coat both sides with combined ingredients, leave to marinate for 2-3 hours or preferably overnight in the fridge. Grill or barbecue basting and turning frequently for about 20-30 minutes, depending on the thickness of the chops.
SERVES 4.

STEWED PORK

2 lbs. pork stew
Salt and pepper to taste
1 garlic clove minced
4 Tbsps. oil
2 onions coarsely chopped
5 whole cloves
4 sprigs fresh thyme chopped
4 eggplants cut in large cubes
2 large tomatoes coarsely chopped
½ lb. green pawpaw peeled and sliced
2 Tbsps. tomato paste
Dumplings if desired
Salt and pepper pork, rub with garlic. Heat oil in a heavy saucepan, brown pork in batches removing pork as browned. Fry onions and cloves 3-4 minutes. Add the remaining ingredients and water to barely cover. Bring to a boil, reduce heat and simmer till pork is tender. Add dumplings 10 minutes before end of cooking time.
SERVES 4.

The Black "Buck" Pots

OVEN BAKED SPARERIBS - *YES! (They are fantastic on the barbecue, particularly cooked on a good old coal pot)*

2 whole racks pork spareribs	¾ cup ketchup
Salt and pepper to taste	½ cup brown sugar
3 garlic cloves minced	1 Tbsp. soy sauce
Juice from 4 limes	1 Tbsp. grated fresh ginger
½ cup water	

Combine all ingredients except salt and pepper, pour over ribs in a baking pan and refrigerate 3-4 hours or overnight. Salt and pepper ribs and bake in the same pan in a preheated 325F. Oven for 1 hour and 20 minutes or till cooked and tender. SERVES 4.

A true Caribbean feast is incomplete with out a suckling pig. We serve it during the "winter" season at our restaurant. Serve with Golden apple sauce for a good tropical flavour. This dish is traditionally served every Christmas in our home.

STUFFED SUCKLING PIG

1 suckling pig, about 20 lbs.	Salt and pepper to taste
Fresh limejuice	Oil
1 garlic clove cut	1 orange

PREPARE PIG: Rub suckling pig inside and out with limejuice, cut clove of garlic and salt and pepper to taste. Refrigerate overnight.

STUFFING:

1 cup butter	¼ cup fresh parsley minced
1 lb. sausage meat sliced thin	1½ tsps. salt
2 large onions chopped	½ tsp. black pepper
1 garlic clove minced	3 tsps. fresh thyme minced
1 sweet pepper chopped	½ tsp. freshly grated nutmeg
2 stalks celery chopped	½ cup raisins
Small piece hot pepper minced	1 egg beaten
4 Tbsps. rum	**Either:** 4 cups fresh breadcrumbs
1 Tbsp. Worcestershire sauce	**Or:** 2 large packages of "wibix" or "Crix" crackers
1 Tbsp. fresh or dried ginger	1 cup milk

PREPARE STUFFING: Melt butter in a large saucepan, cook sausage slices 3-4 minutes, add onion, garlic, sweet pepper, celery and hot pepper. Cook 5 minutes till onion is soft. Add rum, Worcestershire sauce, ginger, parsley, salt, pepper, thyme, nutmeg and raisins, cook 3-4 minutes longer. Soak breadcrumbs or crackers in milk till softened, drain and discard milk. Add to prepared mixture. Cool completely, add beaten egg and refrigerate stuffing separately.

Stuff pig cavity with stuffing, truss cavity with skewers or sew closed with string. Rub suckling pig all over with oil. Open pig's mouth and place a block of wood (the size of an orange) in it to hold it open. Bake in a preheated 475F Oven for 30 minutes, reduce heat to 350F and continue cooking for 2 hours. Increase heat again to 475F, baste with oil and cook a further 20 minutes or till skin is crisp and meat cooked through. Remove block of wood from the mouth, replace it with an orange before serving.

GOLDEN APPLE SAUCE *(also known as "Mock Apple Sauce")*

Peel and remove flesh from 6 golden apples, place in a saucepan with ½ cup sugar and a dash of cinnamon. Add 2 Tbsps. water and cook till fruit is softened. Puree in blender till smooth.

Oven baked spareribs

A Christmas Suckling pig

Sweet & Sour Pork

The Black "Buck" Pots

Sweet and Sour features often in small premises serving take away lunches. In the Caribbean they are prepared with shrimp, chicken or pork but note the omission of soy sauce showing how we have adapted so many foods.

SWEET AND SOUR PORK

2 lbs. boneless pork stew, salt and pepper to taste

BATTER: made of 1 cup flour, 1¼ cups milk and 1 tsp. of baking powder

VEGETABLES: thinly sliced carrots, sweet pepper, large chunks of onions, pineapple chunks, celery chunks, combination of any or better still a bit of all, small piece hot pepper minced.

1 Tbsp. butter

1 garlic clove minced

SAUCE:

¾ cup vinegar

½ cup or more sugar

⅓ cup ketchup

1½ Tbsps. Worcestershire sauce

Good dash of ground cinnamon

1 tsp. cornstarch dissolved in 1 Tbsp. water

Make sauce: Combine all sauce ingredients in medium saucepan, bring to a boil, lower heat and simmer stirring till thickened.

To cook pork: Salt and pepper pork cubes, dip in batter and deep fat fry till golden and cooked, set aside.

To cook vegetables: Heat butter in large frying pan, add garlic and cook 1 minute. Add vegetables and stir-fry 2-3 minutes.

TO ASSEMBLE: Add pork pieces to vegetable mixture and stir-fry 2-3 minutes, add sauce and heat. Serve immediately.

SERVES 6.

Pork and poultry are so interchangeable in recipes that boneless chicken breasts or turkey breasts may be used in this recipe. Use the small chicken or turkey tenders in the puree.

CALLALOO/SPINACH STUFFED PORK TENDERLOINS

2 pork tenderloins salt and pepper to taste

1 cup chopped callaloo or spinach

2 ice cubes

3 Tbsps. cream

Juice from ½ fresh lime

Grated fresh nutmeg to taste

Salt and pepper to taste

Remove small end tips from tenderloin to make an even sized roast. Split tenderloins in half without cutting right through lengthways and flatten slightly by pounding with a mallet between sheets of waxed paper, salt and pepper open end. Meanwhile cook calaloo in a little water till soft, drain thoroughly. Cool. Blend or process in a food processor: reserved pork tips, callaloo, ice cubes, cream, limejuice and grated nutmeg till pureed. Stuff tenderloins with mixture, close and secure with skewers or toothpicks, reshaping into original shape. Salt and pepper outside of tenderloin, dot with butter and bake in a preheated 400F. Oven for 30 minutes.

If desired make pan gravy with the addition of a little cream and wine for serving.

Spinach may be substituted for the callaloo.

SERVES 4-6.

The Black "Buck" Pots

English roasts feature heavily in Caribbean cookery but their flavour from the original blandness has been changed with the addition of herbs and spices.

ROAST LEG OF LAMB WITH PAN GRAVY

1 leg of lamb, salt and pepper to taste

1 bunch fresh rosemary or 2 Tbsps. dried

1 garlic clove cut in slivers

Preheat oven to 375F. Place lamb in roasting pan and generously sprinkle with salt, pepper and rosemary, patting the ingredients on. Cut little slits into the meat and insert garlic slivers. Bake for 1½ hours or till cooked. Remove lamb to board and let rest while making gravy. To the same pan that lamb was roasted in, add 4 Tbsps. flour and mix to incorporate. Place pan on heat and cook over moderate flame 2-3 minutes, slowly add 2-3 cups water or stock, stirring constantly, adjust seasoning to taste, boil till slightly thickened. If gravy needs more flavour, add a lamb or chicken stock cube. *Traditionally served with pan roasted potatoes and mint sauce.*

TO PAN ROAST POTATOES: peel and wash 8-10 English potatoes, place around roast before putting in the oven. SERVES 6-8.

Nothing beats a good hearty Caribbean lamb stew. Add dumplings of choice- see index and garnish with chopped parsley or chopped chive.

LAMB STEW *(This one is for my best friend JUDSY! I always prepare this for her when she comes to Barbados)*

2 lbs. lamb stew meat, salt and pepper to taste

2 Tbsps. oil

1 onion coarsely chopped

2 garlic cloves minced

2 Tbsps. fresh thyme minced

1 Tbsp. Worcestershire sauce

2 onions quartered

2 tomatoes coarsely chopped

2 carrots sliced

2 potatoes quartered

Salt and pepper meat and set aside. Heat oil in a large saucepan, add lamb by pieces and cook till browned, removing browned meat and continuing till all the meat has been browned. To same saucepan, add chopped onions and fry 3-4 minutes, add garlic, cook 1 minute, return lamb to saucepan, add remaining ingredients except potatoes, cook 4-5 minutes stirring. Add 2 cups water or stock. Cook 1 hour till lamb is tender. Add potatoes, cook 20 minutes more. SERVES 6.

Lebanese influenced - try skewering alternately with chunks of tomato, sweet pepper, onions and meat.

LAMB KEBABS

4 lbs. boneless lamb cut into 1" cubes

¼ cup olive oil

3 cloves garlic minced

2 Tbsps. fresh limejuice

¼ cup fresh mint chopped

½ cup plain yoghurt

Whisk together the oil, garlic, lime juice, mint and yoghurt. Marinate the lamb in this mixture overnight in the refrigerator. Place on skewers and grill or barbecue on 5-8 minutes per side basting often. SERVES 8.

The Black "Buck" Pots

Lamb Roast

Lamb Kebabs

Roast beef with all its traditional trimmings

The Black "Buck" Pots

English influenced, we traditionally still serve a roast on Sundays when the whole family gather together to share the meal and companionship.

ROAST BEEF

3-4 lbs. roast beef - *The tenderer the better, I often use a local beef tenderloin.*

2 Tbsps. each fresh rosemary and thyme chopped.

Salt and lots of freshly ground black pepper to taste

4 Tbsps. corn oil-only if meat has no fat as is most cases with local meat

Rub oil all over meat if necessary, sprinkle evenly with rosemary, thyme, salt and lots of black pepper, rubbing everything in well into the meat to adhere. Place in large oiled roasting pan and set aside while preheating oven to 475F.

ROAST POTATOES

Peel 12 large English potatoes, cut in half, and place around roast beef.

YORKSHIRE PUDDING

1 cup of flour

1 cup of milk

¼ cup of water

Pinch of salt

1 tsp. oil

2 large eggs.

Combine all ingredients and whisk till lump free, I find using a large 4 cup glass measure ideal for this as it can then pour into the individual muffin pans easily. Set aside at room temperature for at least 1 hour.

NOW TO PUT THE MEAL TOGETHER - Place a teaspoon of oil in each section of a 12 muffin cup pan. Place pan unfilled in oven to preheat pans.

Place meat and potatoes in a preheated 475F oven with a meat thermometer inserted in the thickest part of the roast. Cook till thermometer registers rear, about 25 minutes for tenderloin, longer for a larger sized roast. Remove roast from pan, place on a serving dish and return potatoes to the oven. reduce oven temperature to 400F.

Whisk the Yorkshire mixture and pour evenly into the heated muffin pan and return to the oven. Cook till Yorkshire puddings are puffed and golden and potatoes cooked, approximately 20-30 minutes longer.

MAKE PAN GRAVY

Remove potatoes from roasting pan and place on platter around beef. To pan add oil if necessary and brown ¼ cup of flour into the pan juices, stirring in brown bits from the bottom. Add 3 cups water or beef stock, stirring constantly and cook till slightly thickened. Add beef cube- if needed for good strong tasting beef gravy. SERVES 6.

SERVE with a nice simple crisp cooked vegetable, freshly prepared hot mustard and or horseradish sauce.

TIPS for Entertaining - judge meat at about 4ozs. per person. Use a meat thermometer for perfect results. Plan on 1 large or 2 small potatoes per person and offer a rice dish as well. Plan on at least 2 Yorkshires per person, recipe can be doubled, trippled etc.

MYTH - Roast beef can be prepared several hours in advance. Cook till slightly under your required doneness, let sit for half an hour, slice and set on serving platter. Let us face it, by the time the roast is brought to the table, carved and everyone served, the meat is entirely at room temperature anyhow. THE SECRET IS TO SERVE YOUR GRAVY PIPING HOT! When poured over the meat it reheats the thin slices of roast.

CARIBBEAN SHEPHERD'S PIE WITH YAM TOPPING

1 lb. minced beef, salt and pepper to taste
1 Tbsp. oil
1 large onion chopped
2 garlic cloves minced
1 tsp. fresh thyme minced
Small piece hot pepper minced
1x 16 oz. tin tomatoes coarsely chopped, liquid reserved
1 tsp. Worcestershire sauce
1 tsp. chili powder
Cooked yam mashed with butter, milk, salt and pepper
Grated cheddar cheese for topping

Heat oil in a large frying pan. Add onion and cook 3-4 minutes, add garlic, thyme and cook 1 minute. Add beef and cook stirring till meat is browned. Add hot pepper, tomatoes and their liquid, Worcestershire sauce and chili powder. Cook 30 minutes or till sauce is slightly thickened. Place mixture is casserole dish, top with mashed yam and cover yam with grated cheese. Bake in a preheated 375F oven for 20-30 minutes or till top is golden and pie is heated through. SERVES 4.

One dish, many flavours! I served this for one of my father's birthday parties using halved coconut shells as my dishes. Guests helped themselves with two or three different condiments then returned for more servings adding different condiments each time and thus creating a whole new flavour with each new helping. The coconut shells were the talk of the town!

CURRIED BEEF DINNER *(Caribbean style)*

2 lbs. stew beef
3 Tbsps. oil
3 large onions coarsely chopped
2 garlic cloves minced
¼ tsp. each ground clove and cinnamon
1 Tbsp. fresh grated ginger
½ small hot pepper minced
3 Tbsps. curry powder
1 tsp. each turmeric, cumin seed and ground coriander
2 Tbsps. tomato paste
1 cup fresh or tinned coconut milk
Water to just cover
Cooked fluffy white rice

CONDIMENTS: Small bowls filled individually with: grated toasted coconut, sliced bananas, raw chopped onion, raisins, a variety of chutneys, chopped peanuts, diced cucumbers, chopped tomatoes, diced pineapple, chopped sweet peppers etc. Let your imagination flow!

Heat oil in a large saucepan, add onions and fry for 2-3 minutes, add garlic, clove and cinnamon, ginger, hot pepper, curry powder, turmeric, cumin and coriander and fry for 2-3 minutes more. Add beef and brown in the curry mixture. Add tomato paste and water to just barely cover. Bring to a boil, lower heat and simmer for 1½ hours or till meat is tender. Add coconut milk and cook for 10 minutes longer.

TO SERVE: Place large bowl of plain, fluffy white rice in center of table and beef curry in similar dish. Use the individual bowls to surround the meal and allow guests to help themselves to rice, top with curry and as many garnishes as they wish. SERVES 6.

Caribbean Curried Beef dinner with accompaniments

Steak & Kidney Pie Caribbean style

Stewed Kidneys a New Years tradition in our family

The Black "Buck" Pots

BEEF STEAK AND KIDNEY PIE *(An English inherited dish but spiced up to suit our tastes)*

1 lb. beef kidneys, cleaned and cut into cubes
1 Tbsp. Angostura bitters
1 small onion chopped
½ tsp. dried rosemary
Salt and pepper to taste
Combine above ingredients and leave to marinate overnight in refrigerator.
1 lb. beefsteak cut in cubes
1 Tbsp. Worcestershire sauce
1 onion chopped
1 garlic clove minced
2 tsps. fresh thyme minced
Small piece hot red pepper minced
Salt and pepper to taste
Combine above ingredients and leave to marinate overnight in refrigerator.
¼ cup butter
Heat butter in a large heavy saucepan, drain beef reserving marinade. Fry beef cubes till browned, remove from pan and return to marinade. To same saucepan add the kidneys along with their marinade and cook till just beginning to colour, return beef and marinade along with ½ cup water or beef stock and cook for 30-40 minutes or till beef is tender. Place in deep pie dish, cover top with puff or flaky pastry and bake in a preheated 400F. Oven for 20 minutes, reduce heat and bake for 10 minutes more or till pastry is cooked. SERVES 6.

Kidneys are traditionally served for BREAKFAST in our family every New Year's Day at my mother's and featured regularly for a Sunday after church brunch at my Aunt's home in Trinidad. Now I swear that my Auntie Joan makes the best stewed kidneys but when asked for her recipe she just laughs and says that she throws in whatever is available in the seasoning side and her secret is adding about a pot spoon full of ketchup which I do not add to mine. What is a pot spoon? She cannot say! Just add to taste for her version. Here is my version.

STEWED KIDNEYS

2 beef or veal kidneys
Salt and pepper to taste
2 onions chopped
2 garlic cloves minced
2 tsps. fresh thyme
½ tsp. fresh marjoram
Small piece hot pepper minced
2 Tbsps. dry sherry
1 Tbsp. each Angostura bitters and Worcestershire sauce
3 Tbsps. butter
POTSPOON of ketchup if liked
Remove fat from kidneys and cut into segments. Place in salted water for 10 minutes. Drain, place kidneys in a glass dish and combine with all other ingredients except butter. Leave to marinate for a few hours or preferable overnight in the fridge. Heat butter in a heavy black iron pot till browned and bubbles subside. Add all of kidney mixture including marinade, cook stirring 3-4 minutes. Add ketchup if liked. Lower heat and cook adding a little water if needed 30-40 minutes or till kidneys are cooked and gravy is thick. Adjust with salt and pepper to taste and serve over hot toast. SERVES 6-8.

The Black "Buck" Pots

BEEF STEW *(The king of all stews, known simply as a Bajan Brown Stew)*

2 lbs. stew beef
3 onions chopped
2 garlic cloves minced
1 Tbsp. fresh minced marjoram
3 Tbsps. each fresh minced thyme and parsley
¼ cup chopped chives
4 carrots sliced
Piece of hot pepper minced
2 Tbsps. Worcestershire sauce
2 Tbsps. oil
4 Tbsps. sugar
Salt and pepper to taste

Marinate beef with onions, garlic, marjoram, thyme, parsley, chives, carrots, hot pepper and Worcestershire sauce for at least 1 hour or preferably overnight in the fridge. Heat oil in a heavy, preferably black iron "buck" pot, add sugar and cook for 3-5 minutes or till a dark caramelized colour, watch carefully and do not allow to burn or stew will be bitter. Add beef and marinade and cook stirring till beef is coated and browned. Add about 4 cups water, salt and pepper to taste, bring to a boil, lower heat and simmer 1½ hours or till beef is tender. *30 minutes before serving time, cubed peeled potatoes may be added, dumplings as well or mixture may be thickened with a little flour and butter kneaded together.*
SERVES 6.

LIVER and BACON

2 liver steaks
Salt and pepper to taste
1 Tbsp. Worcestershire sauce
¼ cup milk
1 tsp. fresh thyme minced
4 bacon slices cut in 4
2 large onions cut in rings

Season liver with salt and pepper, Worcestershire, milk and thyme and leave for 1 hour. Fry bacon in heavy saucepan till almost crisp, remove bacon and set aside to drain. In same fat, fry onion rings 4-5 minutes, remove from pan and set aside. Fry liver and seasonings in same saucepan turning once for 5 minutes per side or till cooked to desired doneness. Serve liver sprinkled with bacon and onions.
SERVES 2.

I love this dish accompanied by a good mashed yam and a side dish of lots of sliced fried onions with pieces of bacon.

FRIED LIVER

4 liver steaks trimmed
1 Tbsp. Caribbean "seasoning"- *see recipe in index*
Flour, salt and pepper to taste.
1 egg beaten with 2 Tbsps. milk
Dry breadcrumbs to coat

Cover liver with "seasoning". Leave for 30 minutes. Dredge in flour mixed with salt and pepper, then in egg mixture and finally in breadcrumbs. Fry till golden. SERVES 4.

The Black "Buck" Pots

The King of all stews, known simply as a Bajan Brown Stew

The Black "Buck" Pots

Creole Tripe in calabash bowls

The Black "Buck" Pots

Both oxtail cut up into serving portions and tongue are prepared this way. Cook the tongue whole or oxtail pieces in a pressure cooker for about 20 minutes. FOR TONGUE, remove pan from heat, reduce pressure by placing pan under running water, remove lid, cool tongue slightly and peel off skin, return to pan, and pressure cook 40-45 minutes more or till tongue is soft. Slice the tongue to serve.

OXTAIL or TONGUE STEW

2 oxtails, cut into 1" pieces or 1 tongue left whole

Salt and pepper to taste

¼ cup oil

4 Tbsps. brown sugar

2 large onions coarsely chopped

3 garlic cloves minced

2 celery ribs chopped

1 sweet pepper chopped

Piece hot pepper minced

3 sprigs fresh thyme

1 sprig fresh marjoram

1x16 oz. tin tomatoes with liquid

1 Tbsp. Worcestershire sauce

Salt and pepper meat. Heat oil in a pressure cooker, add sugar and cook 3-4 minutes till caramelized, add meat, cooking till coated with caramel. Add onions, garlic, celery, sweet and hot pepper, thyme and marjoram and cook 2-3 minutes, add tomatoes, Worcestershire and about 2 cups water. Bring to pressure and cook 30-40 minutes or till meat is tender. Gravy may be thickened with a little flour and butter mixed together. SERVES 6.

When I cook oxtail stew, I often add dumplings towards the last 15 minutes of cooking.

This recipe makes an excellent soup, cut up the tripe into ½" pieces, add 3 cups beef stock and small diced carrots, celery, yam, eddoes and of course dumplings.

CREOLE TRIPE

3 lbs. tripe, salt and pepper to taste

2-3 Tbsps. oil or butter

2 onions chopped

2 garlic cloves minced

2 tsps. chopped fresh thyme

1 sweet pepper diced

Small piece hot pepper minced

4 tomatoes chopped

1 Tbsp. tomato paste

1 Tbsp. Worcestershire sauce

3 Tbsps. chopped fresh parsley

Wash the tripe in water mixed with limejuice. Salt and pepper tripe to taste. Place in large saucepan with enough cold water to cover, bring to a boil, lower heat and simmer covered for 1½ hours or till soft. Remove tripe, reserving stock, cool tripe slightly and cut into 1" square pieces. Heat oil or butter in a next saucepan, add onions and garlic and fry 3-4 minutes, add thyme, sweet pepper, hot pepper and tomatoes. Cook 10 minutes. Add tomato paste, Worcestershire and the reserved tripe. Cover meat with reserved stock, bring to a boil, reduce heat and simmer 45 minutes to 1 hour. Gravy may be thickened with a little cornstarch dissolved in water. Sprinkle with parsley before serving. SERVES 8.

The Black "Buck" Pots

CURRIED GOAT (*Curried goat is served in most islands with an Indian community; this recipe is famous in Jamaica. Lamb may be substituted*)

2 lbs. goat meat cut up as for stew and preferably with bones left in for added flavour
Salt and pepper to taste
6 blades of chive chopped
6 garlic cloves minced
2 Tbsps. oil
2 onions chopped
4 Tbsps. curry powder
1 tsp. cumin seeds or geera
Small piece of hot pepper minced
2 cups water
4 potatoes, peeled and quartered

Season meat with salt and pepper to taste; add chive, garlic and 1 Tbsp. of the curry powder, leave to marinate several hours or overnight in the fridge. Heat oil in a large saucepan, fry onions till golden, add remaining curry, cumin and fry 2-3 minutes. Add goat pieces, turning to coat with curry and brown, add any remaining marinade, hot pepper and water. Bring to a boil, lower heat and simmer 2-3 hours. Add potatoes and continue cooking 20 minutes or till potatoes are tender.
SERVES 4.

RABBIT STEW CREOLE STYLE

1 rabbit cut into serving pieces
Salt and pepper to taste
3 Tbsps. oil
3 Tbsps. sugar
6 blades chive chopped
2 large onions chopped
3 garlic cloves minced
2 carrots, sliced thin
Rind from ½ an orange
Dash of ground clove
1 tsp. oregano
Small piece hot pepper minced
1 Tbsp. chopped fresh thyme
Juice from 1 orange
1 Tbsp. Angostura bitters
1 cup white wine
2 Tbsps. chopped parsley

Combine chive, onions, garlic, carrot, orange rind, ground clove, oregano, hot pepper, thyme, orange juice and bitters for marinade. Salt and pepper rabbit and add to marinade, leave overnight in refrigerator. Heat oil in a large heavy saucepan, add sugar and cook 2-3 minutes or till mixture browns and caramelizes (be careful not to let it burn or it will be bitter), add rabbit pieces and cook stirring till coated with caramel mixture. Add remaining ingredients from marinade, cook 5 minutes. Add wine, cover pot, lower heat and simmer 1 hour. Sprinkle with parsley before serving. Sauce may be thickened with a little flour and water paste if desired. SERVES 4.
Sometimes I add a few tablespoons of orange liqueur plus a tablespoon of brandy just before serving.

The Black "Buck" Pots

Bamboo Grove in Jamaica

Government Buildings - Bridgetown, Barbados

Carnival colours and movement. Most of the Caribbean islands partake in carnival. Check each individual island for their particular dates

Associated Island Foods

My favourite coast in Barbados - East Coast - Cattlewash

Caribbean flowers Ginger Lillies & Anthuriums

Tropical fruit - Bananas and Mangoes

This chapter contains recipes of food that I personally associate with particular Caribbean Islands. In some instances they actually are or originated from the mentioned island.

PEPPERPOT An original Amerindian dish, excellent for entertaining

Associated Island Foods

GUYANA

PEPPERPOT *(This is an original Amerindian dish. May be frozen. It may also remain out on the counter provided it is brought to the boil every day and great care must be taken to use a clean spoon for stirring with no traces of any form of starch whatsoever or mixture will ferment. Serve with plain boiled rice and or plain boiled sweet potato)*

1 oxtail cut in 1" lengths
2 lbs. cow heel cut in small pieces
2 lbs. pig trotters split
1 lb. salt beef or pig tail
4 lbs. pork stew
4 lbs. beef stew
2 chickens or stewing ducks, cut up
1 lb. salt beef
1 cup cassareep
10 Tbsps. sugar
8 large onions chopped fine
6 cloves garlic minced
SPICES:10 whole cloves, 2 pieces of cinnamon stick, 10 stalks of fresh thyme finely chopped, 3 whole hot peppers, a piece of dried tangerine or orange peel
Salt and pepper to taste
Place oxtail, cow heel, trotters and salt meat in a large saucepan with enough water to cover, bring to a boil, lower heat and simmer for 2 hours, or pressure cook for 1 hour. Skim any froth from stew, add pork, beef stew, chicken, cassareep, sugar, onions, garlic and spices. Bring back to the boil, reduce heat and continue simmering for 2 hours longer or till meats are tender or pressure cook for 40 minutes more. Cover pot tightly, leave overnight, next day, crush the hot peppers in the stew, bring to a boil and simmer for a further hour. Remove whole spices and any bones if desired. Freezes beautifully! SERVES 25.

GARLIC PORK *(Portuguese influence)*
This dish is traditionally served around Christmas time. Eat a lot of parsley followed by a shot of vodka - helps with the garlic breath situation!
2 lbs. very fresh leg of pork
Salt
¼ lb. chopped garlic cloves
3 thick fresh thyme sprigs
5 onions chopped
1 hot pepper chopped
1 Tbsp. salt
2½ cups white vinegar
Cut pork from leg in 1" cubes, clean meat thoroughly. Bring a large pot of water to a boil, scald pork in boiling water by immersing and lifting out immediately in batches. Drain and pat dry. Sprinkle with salt and leave to further dry. Bring a large pot of vinegar to a boil, boil 5 minutes then leave to cool but must be slightly warm to use. Mix garlic, thyme, onions, hot pepper and set aside. Use sterilized clean glass containers with tight fitting lid. Place the tablespoon of salt in the container, fill with a quarter of the pork, third of the garlic mixture and warm vinegar to barely cover. Continue layering in this manner. Cover tightly and leave for 7-9 days. To cook, remove some pork as needed with a clean wooden spoon, place in a heavy saucepan with a little oil and cook till liquid is evaporated and pork browned. Serve with lots of parsley. SERVES 6.

Associated Island Foods

TRINIDAD & TOBAGO

Considered one of TRINIDAD and TOBAGO'S NATIONAL DISHES. This dish is often served on picnics. Wrap the entire saucepan and cover in newspaper or a blanket and it will still be hot at serving time.

I often prepare this dish to the stage just before adding the rice, then I cool it, divide out the chicken pieces into freezer containers, add two cups of liquid from the stew to each container and freeze! Then when unexpected guests arrive as often happens in the islands, I simply defrost my mixture on the stove top and add 1 cup of rice per frozen portion.

So many recipes exist for this dish, just let it be said that they are all correct! It is one of those dishes were everything goes and everything depends on the individual family likes and dislikes.

CHICKEN PELAO

1 chicken cut up into joints
Salt and pepper to taste
¼ cup each rum, Worcestershire and Angostura bitters
2 large onions chopped
4 garlic cloves minced
½ a hot pepper, seeded and minced
1 stalk celery chopped
1 small sweet pepper chopped
2 Tbsps. fresh thyme chopped
2 tsps. fresh marjoram chopped
3 Tbsps. oil
½ cup brown sugar
2 cups rice
3 cups water or chicken stock
½ cup coconut milk
1 cup cooked or tinned pigeon peas
¼ cup raisins
¼ cup sliced olives

Marinate chicken overnight with the salt, pepper, rum, Worcestershire sauce, bitters, onions, garlic, hot pepper, celery, sweet pepper, thyme and marjoram. Heat oil in a large heavy saucepan, add sugar and cook till caramelised or deep brown, being careful not to let the sugar burn or dish will be bitter. Add chicken pieces a few at a time and cook turning till quoted with caramel, remove chicken back to marinate and continue cooking the rest of the chicken till all have been browned. Return all the chicken to the same pan with all of the marinade. Bring to a boil, reduce heat, cover tightly and simmer for 15 minutes. Bring back to a boil, add rice, water or stock. Bring back to a boil again, lower heat, cover and cook 20 minutes. Add coconut milk and pigeon peas, lower heat, cover and cook 5-10 minutes more. Add raisins and olives and continue cooking till water has evaporated about 5 minutes longer.
SERVES 6.

For a special luncheon or dinner party, serve this dish surrounded with little individual bowls of chopped onion, hard boiled eggs, tomatoes, cooked crisp bacon, grated coconut, peanuts and of course various home made chutneys, pepperjelly sauce and a good Caribbean hot sauce. Simply add a garlic bread or some fried bakes and a salad to round off the meal.

PELAO, a must for carrying on picnics

Pastelles - A Christmas special, can also be prepared with chicken or a vegetable filling

PASTELLES *(A Trinidad Christmas specialty with Spanish origins, dough 1 is authentic but dough 2 although not the traditional recipe is an excellent substitute for the corn Masa which is not always available)*

DOUGH 1: 2 cups yellow corn Masa
1 Tbsp. melted butter
¼ cup oil
1 tsp. salt
3½ - 4 cups boiling water

Combine the ingredients and kneed to a soft dough using the smaller amount of water and adding more if necessary.

DOUGH 2: 3 cups yellow cornmeal
6 ½ cups boiling water
½ cup butter
2 eggs beaten
2 tsp. salt

Mix cornmeal with a little of the water to moisten in a large saucepan, slowly the remaining boiling water, stirring continuously till smooth, add salt and butter, reduce heat and cook for 10-15 minutes. Remove from heat, beat in eggs and cool slightly.

FILLING: 2 Tbsps. butter or oil
2 onions chopped fine
2 cloves garlic minced
1 sweet pepper minced
½ a hot pepper minced
1 lb. ground beef
1 lb. ground pork
2 tomatoes chopped
2 tsps. vinegar
4 sprigs thyme chopped
1 beef cube dissolved in 1 cup of water
½ tsp. black pepper
2 Tbsps. Worcestershire sauce plus 1 tsp. white vinegar
12 olives sliced
2 Tbsps. capers drained and chopped
¼ lb. raisins
6 rashers of bacon cut in ½" cubes
12 prepared banana leaves - *see banana leaves in index* or foil

Melt butter in large saucepan, add onion and fry 2-3 minutes, add garlic, sweet and hot pepper and fry 2-3 minutes, add meats and fry till browned, add tomatoes, vinegar, thyme, stock mixture, pepper, and Worcestershire and vinegar. Cover tightly and simmer 20-30 minutes adding a little water if necessary to prevent drying out. Remove from heat, cool and mix in olives, capers, raisins and bacon.

TO PREPARE: Place about 4 Tbsps. of cornmeal mixture on a banana leaf or piece of foil cut 7" square. Flatten mixture, add about 2 Tbsps. meat mixture and fold leaf over into an parcel. Tie with string parcel style and simmer parcels for 1 hour. Makes 16-20 pastelles.

CHICKEN: Substitute beef and pork with 2 lbs. of diced chicken.
VEGETABLE: Substitute meats with 1 lb. chopped dasheen/callaloo, ½ lb. sliced ocroes and ½ lb. diced eggplant.

Associated Island Foods

BARBADOS

SALT FISH and COU-COU- BARBADOS' NATIONAL DISH

Steamed flying fish is also served as an alternative with the cou cou. Quite often this dish is served with pickled cucumber. (Grate cucumber on large side of grater, combine with pickle sauce - *(see recipe in index)* and let sit 1 hour.

CORN MEAL COU COU: Prepare 1 recipe Corn Meal Cou Cou - *see recipe in index.*

SALT FISH STEW

1 lb. salt fish, soaked overnight
2 Tbsps. Butter or sweet oil (olive oil)
2 large onions coarsely chopped
2 garlic cloves minced
2 chives chopped
3 tomatoes chopped
2 tsps. fresh thyme minced
Small piece hot pepper minced
2 cups water
a few dashes of Worcestershire sauce
Salt and pepper to taste.
Remove any bones from fish and shred. Heat butter in a saucepan fry onions for 5 minutes over low heat but do not let brown, add garlic and cook for 2 minutes more. Add chives, tomatoes, thyme and hot pepper. Fry for 5 minutes. Add the water and Worcestershire. Cook about 10-15 minutes longer. Add the shredded salt fish. Cook for 2-3 minutes more. Salt and pepper to taste.
TO SERVE: place a mound of cou cou on serving platter, make a large indentation with a soup ladle or large spoon and pour stewed salt fish with lots of gravy in centre.

STEAMED FLYING FISH

8 prepared flying fish
Salt and pepper to taste
Juice from 1 lime
2 Tbsps. BARBADOS SEASONING - *see index*
2 Tbsps. butter
2 onions chopped
1 garlic clove minced
2 tsps. fresh thyme minced
2 tomatoes chopped
Small piece of hot pepper minced
Dash of Worcestershire sauce
1 cup water or fish stock
Pour lime juice evenly over fish. Let sit 5-10 minutes. Season fish between grooves with Barbados Seasoning, sprinkle with salt and pepper to taste. Heat butter in a saucepan, fry onions 5 minutes, add garlic and thyme, cook 3 minutes, add tomatoes, hot pepper, Worcestershire, water or stock stirring constantly. Cook till slightly thickened about 8 minutes. Roll flying fish inward from the tail end jelly roll fashion, secure with toothpicks. Place fish in sauce, cover and steam over very low heat 10 minutes or till fish are cooked. SERVES 4.

Bajan steamed Flying Fish and Cou Cou

Associated Island Foods

Gros Islet barbecue - St. Lucia

GRENADA & THE GRENADINES

I always associate two particular dishes with Grenada - a good BREADFRUIT OILDOWN - See recipe in index and Callaloo served as a vegetable.

VEGETABLE CALLALO SIDE DISH

2 Tbsps. butter
1 each- onion, sprig of thyme, blade of chive and clove of garlic minced
½ cup coconut milk
18 callaloo leaves cleaned and sliced
Freshly grated nutmeg
Heat butter in a saucepan, fry onion, thyme, chive and garlic 2-3 minutes, add callaloo leaves and fry 2-3 minutes. Salt and pepper to taste. Add coconut milk, lower heat and simmer till coconut milk is absorbed and callaloo is tender. Sprinkle with a little freshly grated nutmeg.
SERVES 4.

ST. VINCENT & THE GRENADINES

Tiny little fish prepared whole

TRI TRI CAKES

½ lb. tri tri, washed and cleaned
½ cup of flour
½ tsp. baking powder
1 egg, lightly beaten
1 tsp. limejuice
2-3 blades of chive
Some fresh thyme, onion and hot pepper minced
Salt and pepper
Combine flour and baking powder in a bowl. Mix in a little water to make a very thick batter, add remaining ingredients, let sit for 5 minutes and deep fat fry by tablespoons in hot oil.
SERVES 4.

ST LUCIA *(A Gros Islet Friday night special)*

BARBECUED CHICKEN OR PORK

1 Chicken cut up or 4 pork chops
1 onion grated
2 sprigs each of fresh thyme and chives chopped

2 tsps. hot pepper sauce
Dash of Worcestershire sauce
¼ cup oil

Whisk the above ingredients except meat together. Pour over meat and marinate overnight. Cook over hot coals basting with the following sauce.

BARBECUE SAUCE

1 Tbsp. oil
1 onion sliced thin
2 cloves garlic minced
1 cup tomato ketchup

1 Tbsp. each Worcestershire sauce, limejuice
2 Tbsps. sugar
1 Tbsp. hot sauce

Heat oil in a saucepan, fry onion 3 minutes, add garlic and fry 1 minute longer, add remaining ingredients and cook till sauce is thickened about 10 minutes. Reserve half of sauce for serving.
Salt and pepper meat, place on hot coals and cook basting with the sauce and turning frequently till done, about 30-40 minutes. Serve with rewarmed barbecue sauce reserved sauce if liked.
SERVES 4.

Associated Island Foods

DOMINICA *(A special breed of frog found in Dominica and Montserrat is used here)*

FRIED FROG LEGS *(Also known as Mountain Chicken or Crapraud)*
Wash and clean 12 frog's legs. Marinate in a mixture of limejuice, salt, pepper, minced garlic, chopped onion, chives, minced hot pepper and fresh thyme for 1 hour. Dip in flour seasoned with salt, pepper and paprika, then in 2 eggs beaten with 2 Tbsps. water and finally in dry breadcrumbs. Let sit 15 minutes to firm coating. Deep fat fry till cooked and golden. SERVES 4.
Alternatively, make a sauce by frying 2 sliced onions in 2 Tbsps. butter till just golden. Add ½ cup milk and a roux of ½ Tbsp. flour mixed with ½ Tbsp. butter, cook till thickened. Salt and pepper to taste. Add chopped fresh parsley and a dash of freshly grated nutmeg. Place sauce on platter, top with frogs' legs. Garnish with lots of freshly chopped parsley.

ANTIGUA & BARBUDA

DOUCANOU - DUCANA
1½ cups flour
¼ tsp. salt
½ tsp. freshly grated nutmeg
1 tsp. Caribbean brown sugar
2 cups each peeled finely grated sweet potato and coconut
1 cup milk
Dash of vanilla extract
Banana leaves singed and cut into 8" squares - **see index.**
Mix the flour, salt, nutmeg and sugar in a mixing bowl. Add the sweet potato and coconut combining well. Gradually add the milk and vanilla to form a soft dough. Place a heaping tablespoon of the mixture on a banana leaf, fold over the leaf tucking in the sides parcel fashion. Tie with soft string. Drop into a large saucepan of boiling water and cook 20-25 minutes.
SERVE WITH SALT FISH STEW - see recipe in index.
SERVES 4

ST. KITTS & NEVIS /ANGUILA

CASSAVA MUSA
This dish is served with stewed salt fish or any steamed saucy fish with lots of gravy. A good accompaniment is slices of peeled avocado.
2 cups cassava meal (finely grated dry cassava)
2 cups water
2 Tbsps. butter
4 okras cut into thin slices
1 tsp. salt
Additional butter for topping
Soak cassava meal in 1 cup of the water for at least 1 hour. Place butter, okras, salt and remaining water in a saucepan and cook 5 minutes. Slowly add soaked meal stirring constantly until thick and smooth. Cover pot and let steam for 10 minutes. Pour into a greased bowl, top with additional butter and serve with stewed salt fish.
SERVES 4.

Associated Island Foods

Doucanou & Salt Fish - Antigua

Associated Island Foods

Game fish, shown with breadfruit chips

MONTSERRAT

GOAT STEW (*Young goat is generally used. Although not readily available in most countries a good piece of mutton with bones is a fair substitute, and as always, add a few dumplings of any variety - see index*)

3 lbs. goat stew meat
Salt and pepper to taste
Flour for dredging
2 cups coarsely chopped onions
4 garlic cloves minced
¼ hot pepper minced
4 blades of chive chopped
1 Tbsp. fresh thyme chopped
1 cup chopped tomatoes
1 cup sliced carrots
4 potatoes, peeled and cubed
4 cups water

Season meat with salt and pepper to taste. Dredge lightly in flour. In a large saucepan brown meat in batches in oil, removing meat when browned. (This should take about five minutes per batch.) When all the meat is browned, fry onion and garlic 3-4 minutes in the same saucepan, then add hot pepper, chives, thyme, tomatoes and return meat to saucepan. Cook 5 minutes. Cover with water, bring to a boil, reduce heat and simmer 1½-2 hours or until meat is tender. Add carrots and potatoes and cook 15- 20 minutes longer. Add dumplings with the potatoes if desired- see index for recipe. Adjust recipe with additional salt and pepper to taste if needed.
SERVES 6.

VIRGIN ISLANDS

(When I think of the Virgin Islands, I think - Game fish!)

Any game fish steak will do, but please slightly undercook the fish, it will continue cooking if left to sit for a few minutes to reach what I term " fishy perfection".

GAME FISH

4 sword fish or any game fish steaks
¼ cup olive oil
2 Tbsps. fresh limejuice
2 Tbsps. freshly grated ginger
¼ cup fresh orange juice
2 Tbsps. soy sauce
1 tsp. sugar
Chopped fresh chives for garnish

Combine oil, limejuice, ginger, orange juice, soy sauce and sugar. Pour over fish steaks and marinade for 1 hour or longer. Salt and pepper steaks. Grill or barbecue turning once and basting frequently for 3-4 minutes per side, depending on size. (Slightly undercook) Let sit 4-5 minutes. Garnish with fresh chives before serving.
SERVES 4.

Try the same marinade, instead of grilling or barbecuing, place fish on a buttered plate that will fit in a Chinese steamer pot. Fill pot to ¼ capacity with water, bring to a boil, lower heat, add steamer with plate of fish, top with additional butter and steam for 20 minutes.

JAMAICA

ACKEE AND SALT FISH

1 lb. boneless salted cod or fish, soaked in water overnight and flaked
2 dozen prepared ackee or 1 tin of ackee drained
2 large onions coarsely chopped
4 chives chopped
1 each fresh small hot pepper and green sweet pepper chopped
2 tsps. fresh thyme chopped
4 tomatoes coarsely chopped
6 bacon slices chopped
Chopped chives or parsley for garnish
Fry bacon in large saucepan, add onion, chives, hot pepper, sweet pepper and thyme and fry for 3-4 minutes, add chopped tomatoes and cook till tomatoes are soft, add ackee and fry for 5 minutes being careful to keep the ackee intact. Add salt fish and cook for 4-5 minutes more. Salt and pepper to taste. Garnish with chives or parsley or a combination of both.
SERVES 6.

This is best served with lots of beastly cold beer to help combat the hot pepper flavour.

PEPPERED SHRIMP

3 lbs. shrimp, cleaned but shells left on
2 Tbsps. olive oil
3 garlic cloves minced
2 Scotch bonnet peppers chopped
2 tsps. salt
2 Tbsps. fresh limejuice
Heat oil in a large saucepan, add garlic and peppers, fry 1 minute. Add salt, shrimp and limejuice. Cook stirring 4-5 minutes.
SERVES 8.

To a Jamaican it is simply not Easter till they have tasted one or more of their 'buns'.

EASTER SPICE BUN

3 cups flour
4 tsps. baking powder
1 tsp. freshly grated nutmeg
1 tsp. cinnamon powder
Pinch of salt
1 egg
2 cups brown sugar
1 cup milk or wine or combination of both
1 cup raisins
1 Tbsp. butter, melted
1 tsp. limejuice
Preheat oven to 350F. about 10 minutes. Grease a loaf tin, line with greaseproof paper, grease again. Combine dry ingredients from flour to salt, set aside. Beat egg, add sugar, butter, milk or wine and lime juice. Pour into dry ingredients and beat till smooth. Add raisins. Pour prepared loaf tin and bake for approximately one hour. As soon as the bun is done, make a glaze by using ½ cup brown sugar and ½ cup water, boil until thick, spread on bun and pop back in oven for about 5 minutes. Yields 1 loaf. **OFTEN SERVED WITH THICK SLICES OF CHEESE.**

Ackee & Salt Fish - Jamaica's national dish

Lobster cakes, served over Coconut Curry Sauce

Associated Island Foods

TURKS & CAICOS ISLANDS

CONCH CURRY

2 conchs, cleaned, pounded and cut into 2" pieces
Salt
Fresh limejuice
4 Tbsps. oil
2 large onions chopped
4 garlic cloves minced
2 tsps. cumin seed
Small piece of hot pepper minced
1 Tbsp. curry powder
2 Tbsps. each chopped fresh parsley and chives
1 tsp. chopped fresh thyme
1x16oz. tin of stewed tomatoes undrained

Combine conch with salt and some limejuice. Let sit 5 minutes. Heat oil in a saucepan, fry onions 4-5 minutes, add garlic, cumin, hot pepper and curry powder, fry 4-5 minutes. Add parsley, chives, thyme and tomatoes. Bring to a boil, reduce heat and simmer 20-30 minutes. Add conch and cook 2-3 minutes.
SERVES 4.

CAYMAN ISLANDS

LOBSTER CAKES

2 Tbsps. butter
½ cup minced onion
½ cup fresh breadcrumbs
2 beaten eggs
¼ cup cream
3 cups coarsely chopped cooked lobster meat
¼ cup finely chopped celery
1 Tbsp. fresh limejuice
¼ cup chopped parsley
½ small hot pepper minced
Salt and black pepper to taste
Flour, eggs and fresh breadcrumbs for coating

Melt butter in a saucepan, fry onion 3-4 minutes till soft, remove from heat and stir in remaining ingredients. Chill for at least 2 hours. Shape into 4" cakes, dip in flour, then beaten egg with a little water and finally in breadcrumbs. Chill 1 hour longer. Fry in a little oil combined with butter turning once. SERVES 4.

DIPPING OR SERVING SAUCE FOR LOBSTER CAKES

1 Tbsp. butter
1 Tbsp. flour
1 tsp. curry powder
1 cup coconut milk
2 Tbsps. chopped fresh basil

Heat butter in a frying pan, add flour and curry, cook 3 minutes over low heat. Slowly add coconut milk, stirring continuously till slightly thickened, add basil, salt and pepper to taste.

Associated Island Foods

BAHAMAS

CONCH prepared in almost every varying form becomes Bahamians National food.

CONCH SOUSE or SALAD

3 conch
½ cup limejuice
Salt and pepper to taste
1 Tbsp. sugar
2 onions minced
1 sweet pepper chopped
1 bunch parsley chopped
Small piece hot pepper minced
Cut conch into very thin slices and pound with a wooden mallet to tenderise.
Place in a bowl with most of the limejuice, reserving about 2 Tbsps. for later use. Refrigerate overnight. Drain the conch discarding the juice, quickly rinse under cold water and add remaining ingredients, adding the reserved lime-juice to taste. SERVES 6.

Serve these with a hot dipping sauce or simply combine a bit of ketchup with some hot sauce.

CONCH FRITTERS

3 cups ground conch
1 cup flour
1 heaping tsp. baking powder
1 onion chopped
½ tsp. each salt and black pepper
Chopped chive, thyme and hot pepper
1 egg beaten
Water to bind batter
Combine all ingredients from conch to egg, mixing well. Add enough water to just bind. Fry in deep fat turning often till golden. SERVES 6.

Gorgeous in its simplicity: but try adding a pinch of garlic, some sliced sweet peppers, julienne carrots - anything goes.

CONCH SAUTE

Meat from 2 conchs
2 Tbsps. butter
1 large onion sliced
2 Tbsps. chopped fresh parsley
Pound conch meat to tenderise, slice into thin pieces. Place in a saucepan just a small amount of water and cook 5 minutes. Drain and reserve. Heat butter in a saucepan, fry onions ill golden, return conch to this saucepan and cook turning till golden. Sprinkle with parsley, salt and pepper.
SERVES 4.

CRACK CONCH

1 tsp. ground allspice combined with ¼ tsp. dry garlic powder and 2 cups dry breadcrumbs
2 lbs. prepared pounded conch, cut into slices or chunks
Seasoned flour for dredging (Salt and peppered flour)
2 eggs beaten with 2 Tbsps. milk
Dip conch pieces in flour, then egg mixture and finally in breadcrumb mixture. Allow to rest for 20 minutes to firm coating. Deep fat fry till golden.

Associated Island Foods

Conch fritters, excellent to snack on with pre dinner drinks

Red and yellow Flamboyant trees

The Sweet Tooth

A selection of prepared pastries and desserts, by kind permission from "FLINDT Patisserie"

What a lovely way to round off your meal with the amazing array of desserts that we produce.

With all the tantalizing fruit that we grow so easily it is just a matter of imagination and substitutions to come up with delights that the world has not yet encountered.

Even a simple Caribbean fruit salad is prepared differently here by the addition of a drop or two of lime juice, rum and aromatic bitters, which enhances the flavour of each individual fruit that make up our tropical meal finale.

Surprisingly, after eating a pot full ('bellyful') of food, we still find space for our sweets and puddings!

The Sweet Tooth

Chocolate Rum Cream Pie, Rum Babas and Crème Caramels

Caramels are served regularly in the Caribbean, so many varieties exist that I recommend experimenting with various alternatives.

CREME CARAMEL

½ cup brown sugar
2 Tbsps. water
2 whole eggs plus 2 egg yolks
1 cup cream

1 tin condensed milk
1 tsp. vanilla
Freshly grated nutmeg

Heat sugar in a heavy saucepan till light golden brown, remove from heat and carefully add the water. (Mixture will splatter so be careful). Place mixture in a tin mold, swirling to cover sides and set aside. Whisk remaining ingredients till blended. Pour over prepared mold, sprinkle top with grated nutmeg. Place mold in a larger baking pan filled with hot water and bake in a preheated 325F oven for 40 minutes. Remove from water, cool and refrigerate overnight before unmolding. SERVES 6.

GINGER CARAMEL: Add ¼ cup very finely grated fresh ginger.

COCONUT CARAMEL: Add 1 cup very finely grated coconut.

ORANGE CARAMEL: Substitute 1cup fresh orange juice for the cream and add zest from 1 orange.

COFFEE CARAMEL: Add 2 Tbsps. instant coffee dissolved in 2 Tbsps. water, omit vanilla and sprinkle with ground cinnamon.

RUM BABAS

Combine: 1¾ cup flour and a scant tsp.of salt
Dissolve: 1 Tbsp. dry yeast in 3 Tbsps. warm water with 1 Tbsp. sugar for 5 minutes
4 eggs
½ cup butter, softened
¾ cup currants soaked in ¾ cup rum (Reserve rum after draining fruit)
Syrup: Boil 2½ cups sugar with 4 cups water till sugar is dissolved about 5 minutes. Add reserved rum plus additional ¼ cup rum.

Place flour mixture in the bowl of a food processor. Add yeast mixture and eggs. Process 2 minutes. Leave the mixture in the processor, cover with a cloth and allow to rise for 45 minutes to 1 hour. Add butter, process 2 minutes. Fold in drained currants. Place mixture in well greased muffin pans , cover with a cloth and let rise for 45 minutes. Bake in a preheated 400F oven for 20-25 minutes. Remove from oven and immediately place babas in rewarmed rum syrup turning till swollen about double their size. Serve warm. MAKES 18-20.

RUM CREAM PIE

8 ½ ozs. chocolate cookies crushed
½ c butter melted
Sprinkle 1 envelope unflavoured gelatin in ¼ cup cold water to soften (5 minutes)
⅓ cup rum
6 ozs. semisweet chocolate, melted and cooled
6 egg yolks
1 cup granulated sugar
2 cups chilled whipping cream

Combine cookies with butter, line a pie dish with mixture pressing firmly. Refrigerate to harden. Microwave gelatin 30-35 seconds to dissolve, add the rum, melted chocolate and cool completely. Beat the egg yolks with the sugar (8 minutes till pale and thick). Fold into the gelatin mixture. With clean beaters whip cream to firm peak stage. Fold in half the cream with the chocolate mixture. Place in pie crust, top with remaining cream. Freeze at least six hours. SERVES 6.

The Sweet Tooth

Claudette Colbert, famous movie star of the 40's-70's, lived in Barbados for most of her life, a friend once asked me to make a dessert for her as a gift and since then, it became a standard order from her household to celebrate her birthdays. We were fortunate to get her old Bajan louvre doors, which were installed at my restaurant "THE COVE", so for our anniversary we prepare this special to celebrate.

CLAUDETTE'S CHOCOLATE MOUSSE CAKE

6 Tbsps. cocoa powder
¼ lb. of butter melted
7 eggs separated
1 cup granulated sugar separated
1 tsp. vanilla extract
⅛ tsp. cream of tartar
Chocolate curls for garnishing

Preheat oven to 350F. Combine cocoa with melted butter, set aside. Whisk egg yolks with ½ cup of the sugar till thick and lemon coloured about 8 minutes. Slowly whisk in warm cocoa mixture, add vanilla and whisk till blended, set-aside. With clean beaters, whisk egg whites with cream of tartar till stiff but not dry, add remaining ½ cup sugar slowly and whisk till thick and glossy. Fold chocolate mixture into the whites lightly but thoroughly. Pour half of batter into an ungreased 9" spring form pan. Bake 35 minutes. (Cover remaining half of batter and refrigerate.) Cool cake completely then top with reserved batter. Refrigerate or freeze. Top with shaved chocolate curls before serving. SERVES 8-10.

CHOCOLATE MOCHA BOMB

8ozs. semi-sweet chocolate
¼ cup rum
¼ cup coffee liqueur
2 tsps. instant coffee
1 cup butter cut into small pieces, room temperature
1 cup sugar
1 tsp. vanilla extract
4 large eggs
1 cup chilled whipping cream
2 Tbsps. icing sugar
Additional 2 tsps. rum

Preheat oven to 350F. Grease a glass pudding dish and line with foil, grease the foil, set aside. Melt chocolate, rum, coffee liqueur and instant coffee in a double boiler over simmering water till chocolate is melted and smooth. Transfer mixture to a food processor or blender, add butter, sugar and vanilla and blend till smooth. Add eggs one at a time blending each before adding the next. Pour into prepared pudding bowl, and bake 45-50 minutes. Mixture will still be very moist in centre. Leave to cool. Refrigerate several hours or up to 3 days. When ready to serve, whip cream to soft peak stage, add icing sugar and rum and whip to stiff peaks. Decorate bomb with cream and serve with the remaining cream. SERVES 8.

CHOCOLATE RUM AND RAISIN ICE CREAM

2 Tbsps. RUM
⅓ cup coarsely chopped raisins
100 grams dark chocolate
1 tsp. vanilla
3 eggs
¼ cup sugar
⅔ cup heavy cream

In a small glass bowl, microwave rum and raisins for 30 seconds, cool. In separate glass bowl, microwave chocolate 1 minute, cool, add the vanilla. Using electric mixer beat eggs and sugar till thick, about 5 minutes, microwave in glass bowl 1 minute, stirring every 20 seconds, cool. With clean beaters of electric mixer, whip the cream to soft peaks. Fold the chocolate into the egg mixture; fold in the cream and finally the RUM raisin mixture. Place in metal loaf pan and freeze 6 hours or overnight. SERVES 4.

The Sweet Tooth

The accompanying photo was the actual cake I prepared for Claudette's 90th. Birthday. After the party, when my platter was returned, I tried quizzing her driver/chauffeur as to who had attended but in typical Barbadian fashion I got no actual confirmation, just a smile when I mentioned some names and a no nod when I mentioned others. Smiles went up for President Ronald Reagan and Frank Sinatra. I like to think that they ate of the exact cake shown!

Pitch Lake cake. Unlike its namesake in Trinidad that keeps replenishing itself, this makes a fast and complete disappearance

The Sweet Tooth

This pudding is named after the famous Pitch Lake in Trinidad.
PITCH LAKE PUDDING

8 ozs. semi-sweet chocolate

1 cup granulated sugar

5 eggs separated

3 Tbsps. rum

1 cup whipping cream

Melt the chocolate and sugar in the top of a double boiler. Beat in the yolks one at a time, remove from heat and stir in the rum. Cool. Whisk egg whites with a pinch of salt till stiff and fold into the cooled chocolate mixture. Whip the cream, fold in half into the chocolate mixture. Place in a pudding bowl, top with remaining cream and chill.

PITCH LAKE CAKE Cut 1 sponge cake - *see recipe in index*, or ready prepared Angel food cake into fingers and alternate layer with the pudding mixture above. SERVES 10.

ICE BOX BASIC RECIPE

1 sponge cake

½ lb. butter

1 cup granulated sugar

4 eggs

1 tsp. vanilla

Cut sponge cake into fingers, moisten with a little rum or liqueur (optional), set aside. Cream butter till light, slowly add sugar and continue beating till smooth. Beat in eggs one at a time, beat in vanilla. FOLD IN FILLING OF CHOICE. Place half of the sponge fingers in a dessert dish, place half the prepared mixture over this, repeat layers and refrigerate overnight. Dessert freezes well and may be made several days in advance, place in refrigerator two to three hours before using.

Dessert may be topped with whipped cream. SERVES 10.

FILLING: CHOCOLATE - Melt ½ lb. good quality dark chocolate, cool and fold in.

      GINGER - Fold in ¼ cup drained chopped ginger in syrup.

      GUAVA - Fold in 1½ cups drained and pureed guava stew plus 1 tsp.limejuice.

      MANGO - Fold in 1½ cups pureed fresh mango plus 1 tsp. limejuice.

      PAWPAW - Fold in 1½ cups pureed fresh paw paw plus 1 tsp. limejuice.

      PINEAPPLE - Fold in 1x16oz. tin well drained crushed pineapple.

MUM's MOCHA PUDDING

Digestive biscuits or sponge cake

Coffee liqueur

¾ cup butter softened

¼ cup evaporated milk

¾ cup sugar

3 egg yolks

2 Tbsps. instant coffee dissolved in 2 Tbsps. water

Line a pie dish with coarsely crushed digestive biscuits or sponge cake. Douse with coffee liqueur and set aside. Cream butter and milk with electric beaters, slowly adding sugar till mixture is thick and sugar is dissolved. Add yolks one by one beating well after each addition. Add coffee and beat till incorporated. Pour over prepared pie dish and refrigerate 3-4 hours or till set. *This dessert freezes well - freeze no longer than two weeks.* SERVES 8.

A must on our menu! We often serve it warm with a scoop of cold vanilla ice cream. Try topping with chocolate sauce or chocolate curls.

COVE FUDGE PIE

2 eggs
1 cup sugar
½ cup butter
3 Tbsps. cocoa powder
¼ cup flour
1 tsp. vanilla extract

Whisk eggs and sugar till thick. Melt butter and cocoa in a small saucepan. Slowly add hot cocoa mixture to eggs beating constantly. Add flour and vanilla. Pour into greased pie dishes and bake in a preheated 350F. Oven for 25 minutes. Centre will be soft. SERVES 8.

FLOATING ISLANDS

1½ cups milk
3 eggs, separated
¼ cup sugar
1 tsp. vanilla essence
Additional ¼ cup granulated sugar
4 Tbsps. guava jelly optional

Scald milk, meanwhile beat the egg yolks and sugar till thick and lemon coloured, slowly add hot milk beating constantly, place mixture in top of double boiler with water in bottom and cook over medium heat stirring constantly till mixture thickens, be careful that mixture does not curdle. Cool slightly, add vanilla and chill in a pie plate. Whip egg whites to stiff peaks, slowly add sugar beating till thick and glossy, drop by spoonfuls over the chilled custard to resemble the islands.

OR drop the meringues by spoonfuls in a shallow baking pan with bottom just covered in water and bake in a preheated 325F. oven for 15 minutes then place on top of custard. Soften jelly by beating with a fork or slightly warming it, drizzle jelly over whites. SERVES 6.

Almost any tropical firm fruit can be substituted for the mangoes.

MANGO TRIFLE

1 sponge cake, cut into large squares
½ cup sweet sherry
3 Tbsps. rum
3 fresh mangoes peeled and diced or 1 tin mangoes diced
¼ cup coarsely halved maraschino cherries
6 egg yolks
2 Tbsps. custard powder
1 Tbsp. cornstarch
3 cups evaporated milk
½ cup condensed milk
1 tsp. vanilla

Sprinkle sponge cake with both the rum and sherry, set aside to absorb the liquor. Dissolve the custard powder and cornstarch in a little of the milk, add remaining milk, condense milk, and egg yolks. Place mixture in double boiler over hot water and cook stirring constantly till mixture is very thick, remove from heat and add vanilla. Place a layer of custard in bottom of bowl, add sponge cake, layer sliced mangoes over and dot with chopped cherries, repeat process ending with custard on the top. Refrigerate for 6 hours or overnight. Before serving, trifle may be decorated with whipped cream and additional sliced mangoes and cherries. SERVES 10.

Cove Fudge Pie

The Sweet Tooth

A Billowy refreshing Lime Meringue Pie

The Sweet Tooth

Always a favourite in the Caribbean, using lime makes the dessert really tart and refreshing. Try topping the meringue with some grated lime zest. <u>Whipped cream may be substituted for the meringue to create a cream pie.</u>

LIME MERINGUE PIE

1 pre-baked pastry shell
1 cup sugar
Pinch of salt
4 Tbsps. cornstarch
1¾ cups water
4 eggs separated
½ cup fresh limejuice
1 tsp. grated lime peel
2 Tbsps. butter
1 tsp. cornstarch
¼ tsp. cream of tartar
8 Tbsps. granulated sugar

Mix the 1 cup of sugar, salt and cornstarch with a little of the water till smooth, add remaining water stirring till combined. Microwave on high stirring every 2 minutes for 7-10 minutes or till thick. Lightly beat egg yolks, pour a little of the hot mixture into the yolks then add the yolk mixture back into the dish stirring till completely combined. Microwave for 2 minutes, whisk in limejuice, rind and butter. Cool slightly and add to prepared crust. Whisk egg whites till stiff with the teaspoon of cornstarch and the cream of tartar, slowly add the sugar and whisk till stiff. Place meringue over lime filling to cover completely, coming right up to the sides of the pastry. Bake in a 325F oven for 20 minutes. *OR cool completely, refrigerate and top with whipped cream before serving.*
SERVES 8.

ALTERNATIVE FILLINGS:

COCONUT MERINGUE or CREAM PIE: SUBSTITUTE 1 cup grated coconut for the lime peel and juice and substitute milk for the water. Add coconut at the beginning with the sugar milk etc in the microwave. Continue as in above recipe, when slightly cool mix in ½ tsp. each vanilla and almond essence. SERVES 8.

ORANGE MERRINGUE PIE or CREAM PIE: SUBSTITUTE 2¼ cups fresh orange juice plus 1½ Tbsps. grated orange rind for the water, limejuice and peel. SERVES 8.

GUAVA PIE

1 recipe for double crust pastry
3 cups, peeled, deseeded and sliced guavas
2 Tbsps. sugar
Juice from 1 lime
Piece of cinnamon stick

Place guavas in a saucepan with the sugar, limejuice, cinnamon and about a ¼ cup of water. Cook till guavas are soft, remove cinnamon. Cool. Cut pastry in half, roll out half of pastry and line a greased pie plate with it. Fill with the guavas, roll out remaining half of pastry and top the pie, pressing edges all around with a fork. Slit top of pie in a crisscross fashion and bake in a preheated 400F oven for 25 minutes. SERVES 8.

This fruit salad dessert is wonderful served with slices of honey toasted sponge cake - see recipe in index for sponge cake.

HONEY TOAST: combine 3 Tbsps. honey with 1 Tbsp. butter. Brush on sponge cake and toast in oven till golden.

TROPICAL FRUIT SALAD

1 banana sliced
2 oranges, peeled and cut into natural segments
1 grapefruit, peeled and cut into natural segments
1 small papaw, peeled and cubed
1 small pineapple, peeled, cored and cut into cubes
1 ripe mango, peeled, seeded and cut into cubes
Juice from ½ a lime
3 Tbsps. honey
Dash of rum
Dash of aromatic bitters

Squeeze limejuice over bananas, place in a fruit salad bowl. Add remaining ingredients, toss and chill before serving. SERVES 6-8.

ORANGE CHIFFON PIE

1 sponge cake sliced
3 Tbsps. orange liqueur
1 cup orange juice plus zest from 1 orange
4 eggs separated
1 envelope unflavoured gelatine
½ cup sugar separated

Line pie plate with sponge cake slices, drizzle with orange liqueur. Place orange juice, egg yolks, gelatine and ¼ cup sugar in a medium saucepan, let rest 5 minutes. Whisk ingredients together and heat over low flame stirring constantly till mixture begins to thicken, add zest and set aside to cool. Refrigerate 5-10 minutes till mixture thickens slightly. Whisk whites adding remaining sugar gradually. Fold into yolk mixture and pile on to sponge cake. Chill 4 hours. SERVES 8.

ORANGE SOUFFLE

3 Tbsps. butter
5 Tbsps. flour
1 cup sugar
Grated rind from 1 orange
⅔ cup fresh orange juice
¼ cup evaporated milk
3 eggs separated

Heat butter in a saucepan, add flour and sugar and cook 1 minute. Combine juice and milk; add mixture in a slow steady stream stirring constantly till very thick. Add orange rind, remove from heat and cool slightly. Preheat oven to 350F. Beat egg whites till stiff, gently fold into orange mixture. Place in a greased soufflé dish and bake for 35-40 minutes. Serve immediately accompanied by rummy orange segments. SERVES 6.

Great on their own , topped with ice cream or as a topping for desserts.
RUMMY ORANGE SEGMENTS: Combine ¼ cup simple syrup - *see recipe in index* with 3 Tbsps. rum. Pour over orange segments and leave to marinate.

Tropical fruit salad

The Sweet Tooth

Rum & Raisin Bread pudding, an old recipe comes back!

Preparing a sour sop cream

The Sweet Tooth

RUM & RAISIN BREAD PUDDING

12 slices bread
Butter softened
$\frac{1}{3}$ cup raisins
$\frac{2}{3}$ cup rum
3 eggs
$\frac{1}{2}$ cup sugar
1 tsp. vanilla essence
1$\frac{1}{2}$ cups milk
1$\frac{1}{2}$ cups cream
$\frac{1}{2}$ tsp. ground cinnamon
Combine raisins and rum in a bowl, let sit 10 minutes, drain, reserving rum.
Butter bread generously and cut into 1" squares, place half in a buttered baking dish, sprinkle with all the raisins, sprinkle with cinnamon, top with remaining bread. Combine reserved rum, eggs, sugar, vanilla, milk, and cream, whisk together. Pour over bread and leave for 30 minutes. Sprinkle cinnamon over top. Bake in a preheated 350F. Oven for 35-40 minutes. SERVES 6.

ISLAND VERSIONS OF BREAD PUDDING

Omit cinnamon and use nutmeg.
Instead of raisins use drained stewed guava cut into small pieces.
Top with meringue after 20 minutes of cooking - *see index for lime meringue.*
Serve over a bed of RUM CREAM if desired.

RUM CREAM

$\frac{1}{4}$ cup brown sugar
1 tsp. cornstarch
$\frac{1}{2}$ cup cream
$\frac{1}{2}$ cup rum
Combine sugar and cornstarch mixture in a small saucepan. Slowly add cream stirring to dissolve cornstarch. Cook over medium heat till thickened. Add rum and cook 1 minute.

COFFEE SHERBET

4 tsps. instant coffee powder
$\frac{1}{2}$ cup icing sugar
1 envelope unflavoured gelatine
$\frac{3}{4}$ cup milk
2 cups cream
$\frac{1}{4}$ cup Tia Maria or any coffee liqueur
Combine coffee, sugar, gelatine and milk in a saucepan. Rest 5 minutes. Place saucepan over medium heat and cook stirring till coffee and gelatine are dissolved. Remove from heat and pour in cream and liqueur. Cool. Freeze till firm about 3 hours. Remove mixture to chilled bowl and mix with beaters till softened and smooth but still frozen. Replace in the freezer and continue freezing for 6 hours or overnight. SERVES 6-8.

SOURSOP CREAM

Pulp from 1 small ripe soursop, peeled, seeds removed , mixed with $\frac{1}{2}$ cup water
1 tin each of evaporated and condensed milk, mixed with 2 tsps. vanilla extract
Beat pulp and water with electric beater, slowly add evaporated and condensed milk. Add vanilla and place in metal loaf pan. Freeze for 2 hours. Whip mixture again and refreeze. SERVES 4.

The Sweet Tooth

COCONUT ICE CREAM
1 medium dry coconut, grated
1⅓ cups milk
½ tin condensed milk
½ tsp. each vanilla and almond essence
Heat coconut and milk to just below boiling point, stir, let sit for 1 hour, place mixture in a cheesecloth and wring out to extract as much liquid as possible, discard coconut. Sweeten with condensed milk and essences and freeze for 2-3 hours, mix with electric beaters again and return to freezer for 6 hours or leave overnight. SERVES 6-8.

TAMARIND SHERBET OR ICE
1 cup water
⅔ cup firmly packed brown sugar
1 cup tamarind pulp
Combine water and sugar in a saucepan, heat over low heat till sugar dissolves. Bring mixture to a boil, boil 5 minutes, remove from heat and add tamarind pulp. Cool, freeze for 3 hours. Place mixture in food processor and mix till smooth but still icy. Refreeze at least 6 hours. SERVES 6.

BARBADOS CHERRY ICE
4 cups Barbados cherries
1 cup or more of granulated sugar
¼ cup water
Dash of fresh limejuice
Wash, remove stems from 4 cups cherries and remove flesh from seeds in large chunks. Bring sugar and water to a boil, cook 5 minutes and allow to cool. Add cherries and lime juice. Add additional sugar to desired sweetness, place in metal ice tray and freeze till firm. SERVES 4.

PASSION FRUIT ICE
12 passion fruit
4 cups water
1½ cups sugar
Bring water and sugar to a boil, stir to dissolve sugar. Cut open passion fruit, remove fruit and place in large jar. Pour syrup over and leave stirring occasionally and pressing on fruit till cooled. Strain reserving a few seeds Freeze 2-3 hours, scoop out of container and beat in blender till smooth but still icy, fold in reserved seeds, return to freezer and freeze till firm. SERVES 6.

TANGERINE ICE
3 cups fresh tangerine juice
1 tsp. grated tangerine peel
1 cup sugar
1 Tbsp. orange liqueur
Mix 1 cup tangerine juice with peel and sugar in a saucepan. Stir over medium heat till sugar dissolves. Remove from heat, add remaining tangerine juice and freeze 3 hours. Whisk mixture with electric beaters till smooth. Return mixture to freezer for 6 hours. SERVES 4.

PAPAYA ICE
Combine in a blender or food processor: 4 cups cubed, peeled, deseeded papaya, 2 Tbsps. sugar, 2 Tbsps. limejuice till smooth. Freeze in metal loaf pan till firm. Reprocess in blender or food processor. Refreeze. SERVES 6.

The Sweet Tooth

Coconut Ice Cream

185

Frozen Lime Cream

Also good as a topping to any fruit salad.
FROZEN LIME CREAM

⅓ cup fresh limejuice
2 cups cream
1¼ cups granulated sugar
2 Tbsps. grated lime rind
Garnish: Lime slices and whole maraschino cherries
In a large bowl, combine all ingredients except garnish and beat with electric beaters till blended and cream is very thick. Pour into 6 individual dessert glasses and freeze overnight. Garnish each with a maraschino cherry and a fresh lime slice if desired. SERVES 6.

GUAVA MOUSSE

1 bottle stewed guavas, drained, reserving syrup
1 pkg. unflavoured gelatine, softened for 5 minutes in reserved guava liquid
¼ cup each limejuice and sugar
½ cup cream
2 egg whites
Chop guavas into small bits, set aside. Heat guava liquid and gelatine till gelatine is dissolved; add to guavas with the limejuice and cool. Whip egg whites with clean beaters till soft peak stage, slowly add sugar and beat till glossy. Clean beaters, whip cream to soft peak stage. Fold guava mixture into egg whites, then fold in cream. Place in bowl and refrigerate till firm. SERVES 6.

GINGER MOUSSE

1 envelope unflavoured gelatin, softened in 3 Tbsps. water
1½ cups evaporated milk
Small piece fresh ginger finely grated about ½" piece
4 eggs separated
½ cup sugar
6 Tbsps. rum
6 ozs. finely chopped crystallized ginger
Scald the milk and fresh ginger, leave 10 minutes. Add the gelatin, beaten egg yolks and sugar. Cook over low heat stirring constantly till a custard is formed. Remove from heat, add rum and set aside to cool. Whip eggs whites till stiff; slowly fold into the custard mixture with the crystallized ginger. Place in a bowl and refrigerate till set. SERVES 6.

GRENADA NUTMEG MOUSSE

2 pkgs. unflavoured gelatin, softened in ½ cup cold water for 5 minutes
6 eggs, separated
1½ cups sugar
1 Tbsp. freshly grated nutmeg
1 tsp. almond essence
2 cups whipping cream
Heat gelatin till dissolved. Cool. Beat yolks with 1cup of the sugar till thick. Add nutmeg and essence, fold in gelatine. With clean beaters whip whites till stiff, slowly add remaining ½ cup sugar and beat till glossy. With clean beaters, whip cream to soft peak stage. Fold yolk mixture into whites, and then fold in cream. Place mixture in a bowl and chill 4-6 hours or overnight. SERVES 8.

This is my Mum's recipe, it is so simple to prepare that I use it as one of my last minute emergency desserts. It is wonderful on its own but can be topped with so many different sauces to create quite an exotic dessert. Besides the fruit sauce recipes given, try some sliced or cubed fresh fruit – anything goes!

COCONUT BLANCMANGE

2 cups prepared coconut milk - **see index** or 1 tin of good quality coconut milk

3 Tbsps. cornstarch or cornflour

3 Tbsps. sugar

½ tsp. vanilla essence

½ tsp. almond essence

In a saucepan mix the cornstarch and sugar, use a little of the coconut milk to make a smooth paste, add the remaining coconut milk, stirring constantly. Place saucepan over medium heat and cook stirring till very thick, remove from heat, cool slightly and add the essences. Pour into a lightly oiled mold, cool completely and chill to set.
SERVES 4.

I always serve my coconut blancmange over a bed of fruit sauce. Try one of these.

Puree one of the following in a blender or food processor then chill before serving. A tablespoon or two of a good quality orange liqueur may also be added.

MANGO: 1 cup mango pulp, ¼ cup sugar plus 1 tsp. fresh lime juice

PASSION FRUIT: ¼ cup passion fruit pulp, ¼ cup water, ½ cup sugar. Save a few seeds to add as this gives a pretty effect.

STEWED GUAVA: 1 cup stewed guava with 1 tsp. limejuice.

BARBADOS CHERRY: 1 cup stoned cherry pulp with ½ cup sugar.

PAW PAW: 1 cup paw paw pulp with ¼ cup sugar and 1 tsp. limejuice.

Top the above dessert with opposing slices of fruit

i.e: Mango sauce with slices of stewed guava

Passion fruit sauce with paw paw slices

Guava sauce with mango slices

Barbados Cherry sauce with mango slices

CRUSTLESS COCONUT PIE

4 eggs

¼ lb. butter softened

½ cup flour

1 cup sugar

1½ cups grated fresh coconut

1 cup coconut milk - **see index** or use a good quality tinned coconut milk

½ tsp. vanilla essence

½ tsp. almond essence

1 cup whipped cream for garnish

1 cup toasted coconut for garnish

Place all ingredients except cream and toasted coconut in a blender or food processor. Blend till smooth and well combined. Pour into a greased pie plate and bake in a preheated 350F. Oven for 1 hour. Cool completely. Top with the whipped cream and sprinkle generously with the toasted coconut. Chill. SERVES 8.

The Sweet Tooth

Typical Vincentian boats - St. Vincent

Caribbean Palm Trees

Within The Brick Ovens

Ruins of an Old Brick Oven at Farley Hill House

Is there anything sweeter or more tempting than driving through a village and picking up the scent of fresh breads and buns baking? Luckily this art form still happens through out the island chain and has not yet been swallowed up entirely by the large commercial bakeries, for hard as they try, they cannot touch the small home owned bakeries for the pleasures that they offer us. Many of these places still produce original and nostalgic loaves for sale.

Brick ovens were to be found in days gone by in kitchens which were usually separated from the main house. Today we have modernized and our kitchens are the focal point and family place for gathering. When driving through the countryside you can still see ruins of such brick oven kitchens.

Traditional Christmas Steamed Pudding

Within The Brick Ovens

CHRISTMAS CAKE *(also known as WEDDING CAKE/ BLACK CAKE/ GREAT CAKE/ FRUIT CAKE)*

Cake:
½ lb butter, room temperature
½ cup brown sugar
4 eggs
2 cups flour
1 tsp. baking powder
1 tsp. dried ginger powder
1 tsp. grated fresh nutmeg
3 tsp. ground cinnamon
½ tsp. ground cloves
½ tsp. ground allspice
2½ tsps. lemon essence
2½ tsps. almond essence
1 tsp. vanilla
¼-½ cup browning - *see recipe for browning*
½ cup rum or brandy
Additional rum or brandy for basting during storage

Fruit:
1 cup raisins
1 cup currants
½ cup candied cherries
½ cup candied citrus peel
1 cup mixed dried fruit
1 cup rum
1 cup sweet sherry or port wine
½ cup brandy

Fruit: Mix all ingredients together and store in an airtight jar for at least 1 month. *(If you do not have a month to spare, soak overnight with the spices and essences called for in the cake recipe)*. Grind fruits reserving liquid, add back liquid to ground fruit.

Cake: Preheat oven to 250F. Line a 10" round deep cake pan with two layers of waxed paper, greasing both layers. In a large bowl cream together the butter and sugar till light and fluffy. Add eggs one at a time beating well between each addition. Sift the flour, baking powder and spices if not used in the soaking. By hand, fold in the fruit alternatively with the flour and essences. Add browning to a deep brown colour. Place mixture in prepared baking pan and cook for 3-4 hours or till cake tests done. Remove from oven, pierce with a skewer and pour the ½ cup of rum or brandy over the cake while still warm. Wrap cake in several layers of wax paper then in foil and store for a month for best flavour. During the month, skewer again and pour rum or brandy over, rewrapping as previously..
This cake is usually iced with almond paste and then a royal icing.

CHRISTMAS STEAMED PUDDING *(A vegetarian's delight - NO SUET!)*

Use the above recipe but place mixture in a greased pudding bowl, cover with several sheets of waxed paper and tie with string. Steam over simmering water 2-3 hours or till toothpick inserted in centre comes out clean. Serve warm with Hard Sauce.
I often have to prepare a lot of these in my catering, I fill large baking pans with boiling water, place several puddings in the pan, cover the entire outer pan with foil and bake-steam in a 300F oven for the time required.

HARD SAUCE

⅓ cup butter room temperature
1 cup icing sugar
4-5 Tbsps. rum or brandy
Cream butter with electric beaters till light and fluffy. Slowly add icing sugar and continue beating. Add rum or brandy and beat till blended in.

BANANA CAKE

2½ cups flour
2½ tsp. baking powder
½ tsp. baking soda
½ tsp. salt
Spice: ½ tsp. each nutmeg and cinnamon
½ cup shortening
1¼ cups sugar
2 eggs
1 tsp. vanilla
2½ Tbsps. milk
4 mashed overripe bananas

Sift flour, baking powder, soda, salt and the spices. Cream shortening adding sugar gradually and mix till light and fluffy. Add eggs one at a time beating well after each addition. Add vanilla. By hand stir in alternatively the banana and milk with the flour mixture. Pour into 2 greased 9" cake pans and bake in a preheated 375F. Oven for 25-30 minutes or till tested done.

CARIBBEAN CAKE AND ITS VARIATIONS *(Great served on its own or frosted with one of the icings - see index)*

1½ cups flour
2½ tsps. baking powder
1 tsp. salt
¾ cup granulated sugar
½ cup corn oil
6 egg yolks (reserve whites)
¾ cup water or liquid according to variations
1 tsp. vanilla or essence according to variations

Place all the above ingredients in a large bowl in the order listed, mix with electric beaters for 1 minute or till smooth, set aside.

½ tsp. cream of tartar
¾ cup granulated sugar

Beat whites with cream of tartar till soft peaks form, add sugar gradually and continue beating till stiff peaks form. Gently fold into prepared batter. Place mixture in an ungreased 10" baking pan and cook at 350F. for 1 hour or till cake tests done. Remove from oven, invert still in pan over a cake rack and allow to cool completely before turning out.

COFFEE VARIATION: Omit vanilla, replace liquid with ¾ cup cooled strong coffee or 3 tsps. instant coffee dissolved in ¾ cup of water. *Wonderful with chocolate icing- see index*

GINGER VARIATION: Steep 2 ozs. fresh ginger in ¾ cup hot water for 1 hour, process mixture in blender or food processor. Try frosting with lime icing - *see index.*

LIME VARIATION: Use juice and rind of 2 limes, make up the remaining liquid with water, omit vanilla. Try frosting with lime icing - *see index.*

ORANGE VARIATION: Use ¾ cup orange juice instead of water and substitute the vanilla with 1 Tbsp. grated orange rind. Try frosting with orange icing - *see index.*

Caribbean Orange Cake

Coconut Turnovers and Sponge cake

Within The Brick Ovens

DUNDEE CAKE WEST INDIAN STYLE *(Best allowed to mature for a few days)*

1 lb. flour
2 tsps. baking powder
1 lb. butter
1 lb. sugar
10 large eggs
¾ lb. each dried fruit as follows: prunes (cut in quarters), citrus peel, and raisins
½ lb. each chopped fruit as follows: currants, cherries (use both green and red)

1 tsp. vanilla
1 tsp. freshly grated nutmeg
Dash of Angostura bitters
¼ cup rum

Sift flour and baking powder, set aside. Whisk butter till light and fluffy, slowly add sugar and whisk till dissolved, add eggs one at a time beating well after each addition. By hand fold in the flour and fruit along with the vanilla, nutmeg, bitters and 1 Tbsp. of the rum. Pour into a well greased large bundt pan and bake in a preheated 350F.oven for 1½ -2 hours or till cake tester comes out clean. Cool slightly, prick all over with a skewer and pour the remaining rum over. Cool completely. MAKES 1 cake.

The scent of these as you pass a home bakery is enough to convert anyone who does not enjoy coconut.
COCONUT TURNOVERS

BUN:
1 Tbsp. dry yeast
1 cup warm milk
1 cup butter
2 eggs
4 cups flour
1 tsp. salt
3 Tbsps.sugar

FILLING:
1 dried coconut grated
1½ cups sugar
¼ cup water
1 tsp. almond extract
½ tsp. ground allspice
Pinch of cinnamon
Additional egg beaten and sugar to coat

Prepare filling: Cook coconut, sugar and water till thick and syrupy. Remove from heat, add almond extract, allspice and cinnamon. Cool.

Meanwhile dissolve yeast in milk and leave for 10 minutes. Cream butter then add eggs. Combine flour, salt and sugar, add yeast and butter mixture and knead into a soft dough adding more flour only if necessary. Place dough in a large greased bowl and leave to rise for 30 minutes covered with a clean cloth. Cut dough in quarters, roll into a rectangles, place quarter of filling down long side and roll up jellyroll fashion. Repeat with remaining dough. Cut each into 4" logs and place side by side, (leaving a 1" space between each one) on greased baking pan. Cover with same cloth and allow to rise for 20 minutes. Brush with beaten egg, sprinkle with sugar and bake in a preheated 425F. Oven for 20 minutes or till cooked and golden.

This recipe can be used to make sponge loaves, sponge rolls or as a sliced and used as a base for many desserts.
MRS. MEDFORD'S SPONGE CAKE

5 large eggs
1 cup granulated sugar
1 cup flour sifted
½ tsp. each almond and lemon essence
Additional granulated sugar.

With electric beaters beat eggs and sugar for 10 minutes. Add essences and gently fold in flour. Place mixture in a well greased and floured large cake pan, sprinkle with granulated sugar and cook in a preheated 350F. Oven for 35-40 minutes or till cooked. Cool inverted on baking rack in pan. MAKES1 large cake.

Within The Brick Ovens

All of these breads are fabulous toasted and spread with butter.

GINGER BREAD

2 cups flour	3 eggs
½ cup brown sugar	½ cup molasses
1 tsp. baking soda	1 cup milk with 1 tsp. limejuice added
½ tsp. salt	½ cup melted butter
2 tsps. ground ginger powder	Sugar
½ tsp. each ground cinnamon and cloves	

Combine flour, sugar, baking soda, salt, ginger, cinnamon and cloves in a large bowl. In a separate bowl, beat eggs till thick and creamy, add molasses slowly then add milk mixture. Beat in half the flour mixture, beating well. Add remaining flour and when it is incorporated, beat in the butter. Pour into greased 9" square pan, sprinkle top with sugar and bake in a preheated 350F. Oven for 40 minutes.

COCONUT BREAD

1½ lb. flour	2 eggs
4 tsps. baking powder	1 cup of milk
1½ lb. flour	1 tsp. vanilla
1 tsp. ground cinnamon	1 cup raisins
½ tsp. ground clove	1 large grated coconut
¼ lb. butter	Additional sugar
¾ lb. sugar	

Line a loaf pan with wax paper and grease, set aside. Sift flour, baking powder and spices, set aside. Cream butter and sugar till light and fluffy, add eggs one at a time beating well after each addition. Add vanilla to milk and add alternatively with the flour mixture. Fold in raisins and coconut. Sprinkle top with sugar and bake in a preheated 350F. Oven for 1 hour.

SWEET PUMPKIN BREAD

2 cups pumpkin peeled and finely grated	1½ tsps. salt
3 cups sugar	1 tsp. cinnamon
⅔ cup water	½ tsp. ground fresh nutmeg
1 cup oil	2 tsps. baking soda
4 eggs beaten	2 cups raisins
3½ cups flour	

Place all ingredients except raisins in a food processor or blender, blend till smooth. Fold in raisins. Pour into 2 large greased and floured loaf pans and bake in a preheated 350F. Oven for 1 hour or till loaves test done.

BRENDA'S BANANA BREAD

1¾ cups flour	⅓ cup shortening
1¼ tsps. baking powder	⅔ cup sugar
½ tsp. baking soda	2 eggs slightly beaten
¾ tsp. salt	3-4 over ripe bananas, mashed

Sift together flour, baking powder, baking soda and salt.

Cream shortening, adding sugar gradually, continue beating till light and fluffy. Beat in eggs. Add flour mixture alternatively with banana by hand, mixing only till just combined. Place in a well greased loaf pan and bake 350F Oven for 1 hour.

Coconut bread

Cassava Pone

Within The Brick Ovens

CASSAVA PONE

4 cups very finely grated cassava
1 cup butter, melted
1 cup sugar
2 cups milk
½ tsp. grated dried ginger
½ tsp. grated allspice
1 tsp. ground cinnamon
Dash of freshly grated nutmeg
1 cup very finely grated coconut
2 tsps. vanilla essence
1½ tsps. baking powder or 2 eggs well beaten
Squeeze as much liquid out of cassava. Discard liquid. Combine cassava with all other ingredients and mix well. Pour mixture into well greased baking dish and bake in a preheated 350F. Oven for 1-1¼ hours or till mixture is golden and cooked.

CORNMEAL PONE

1cup corn meal
¼ cup flour
¼ cup sugar
2 tsps. baking powder
1 tsp. mixed dry spice
4 Tbsps. butter
½ tsp vanilla
1 coconut very finely grated
¼ lb. very finely grated pumpkin
Milk to mix
Combine corn meal, flour, sugar, baking powder and spice. Rub in butter to resemble crumbs. Add vanilla, grated coconut and pumpkin with just enough milk to form a thick batter. Pour in to a well greased baking dish and bake in a preheated 350F Oven for 1 hour.

SWEET POTATO PONE

4 cups finely grated sweet potato
1 tsp. dried ginger
4 Tbsps. sugar
4 Tbsps. butter melted
1 tsp. cinnamon
1 coconut grated finely
Dash of ground cloves
¼ cup raisins
1 Tbsp. molasses
½ cup milk
Combine all ingredients mixing well, place in a greased baking pan. Bake in a preheated 350F. Oven for 1 hour.

CONKIES

¼ cup brown sugar

¾ lb. pumpkin grated

2 medium sweet potatoes grated finely

1 tsp. each allspice, cinnamon and almond essence

¼ cup each raisins and flour

1 cup coarse corn flour (Not cornstarch but of a coarsely ground cornmeal)

⅔ cup shortening melted

½ cup milk

Prepared banana leaves - *see index*

Combine all ingredients except banana leaves mixing really well. Place a generous tablespoon of mixture on an 8"square banana leaf, fold into a parcel shape and tie with string. Place water in a large saucepan to 2" depth. Put a rack in the saucepan, top with leftover banana leaves, carefully place the conkies on the rack and top with more banana leaves. Cover pan, bring to a boil, lower heat, cook for 1 hour. Remove from pan and cool. Serve in the banana leaves. SERVES 12.

HOT CROSS BUNS *(Hot cross buns are always served at Easter time in the islands)*

1 Tbsp. yeast

1 tsp. flour

1 tsp. sugar

1cup warm milk

4 cups flour

1 tsp. salt

½ tsp. mixed spice

½ tsp. cinnamon

¼ tsp. ground fresh nutmeg

4 Tbsps. sugar

4 Tbsps butter

4 Tbsps. each sultanas and currants

1 egg lightly beaten

Combine yeast with the tsp. of flour, sugar and warm milk. Let rest 10 minutes. Sift together the flour with the salt, mixed spice, cinnamon, nutmeg and sugar into a large bowl. Cut in the butter. Blend egg with yeast mixture and blend with the flour till well mixed and a dough is formed. Leave to rise in a greased bowl for 1 hour. Remove from bowl and kneed well. Cut into 18 pieces and form into round buns, place on greased baking sheet and rest covered with a tea towel for 20-25 minutes. Bake in a preheated 400. F Oven for 15-20 minutes. Cool and glaze with icing sugar and water in the form of a cross. MAKES 18 BUNS.

ROCK CAKES

½ lb. flour

2 tsps. baking powder

Dash of salt

¼ tsp. ground dried ginger

⅓ cup sugar

4 Tbsps. butter

1 egg, lightly beaten

Milk if necessary

¼ cup raisins

2 Tbsps. mixed candied peel

Sift flour, baking powder, salt, ginger and sugar, add butter and rub in as if making pastry. Add egg and milk if needed to just bind ingredients. Fold in fruit. Place by large tablespoonfuls on greased and floured baking sheet and bake in a preheated 375F. Oven for 15-20 minutes.

MAKES ABOUT 10 CAKES.

Within The Brick Ovens

Conkies, traditionally served in the olden days on Guy Fawkes Day but now on Independence Day in Barbados

Within The Brick Ovens

Barbadian Salt Breads

Within The Brick Ovens

Known as HARD ROLLS in St. Kitts,
MASTIFF BREAD in Dominica
SALT BREADS in Barbados, the basic recipe is similar.

SALT BREADS *(top with a piece of coconut leaf for a genuine effect)*

1 pkg. yeast
2 tsps. brown sugar
3 cups warm water, separated
3 lbs. flour
3 tsps. salt
3 Tbsps. lard or butter

Dissolve the yeast and sugar in 1 cup of the water in a large bowl, let rest for 20 minutes or till foamy. Add the flour, salt and lard or butter with remaining warm water to make a soft dough. Knead on a lightly floured surface for 10 minutes till smooth and not sticky. Place in a clean greased bowl and cover with a cloth, let rise 1 hour or till doubled in size. Punch dough down, knead lightly on a floured surface and shape into 10-12 bun shapes. Place buns about 3" apart on a well greased baking sheet, cover with a cloth and allow to rise 30-45 minutes more or until doubled in bulk. Preheat oven to 450F. and bake for 15-20 minutes for buns or 35-40 minutes for loaves or till golden and breads sound hollow when tapped at the bottom.

HOPS *(Trinidad)*

2½ cups warm water
2 tsps. sugar
1 Tbsp. dry yeast
1 Tbsp. shortening melted
8 cups flour
2 tsps. salt

Combine warm water, sugar and yeast in a in a large bowl and rest for 10 minutes. Add the shortening to the yeast. Combine the flour and salt. Add half the amount of flour to the yeast mixture, combining well, rest for 30 minutes. Add remaining flour and knead to a stiff dough, pulling and stretching the dough as you knead. Rest for 30 minutes. Cut dough into 2½-3 ozs. balls, place on a greased baking tray and let rise for 3-4 hours. Bake in a preheated 350-400 F. oven for 20 minutes. Cool slightly then return to oven for a further 5 minutes to crisp crust.

MASTIFF BREAD

1 Tbsp. dry yeast
2 tsps. sugar
4 lbs. flour divided
4 cups warm water
2 tsps. salt
¼ lb. shortening

Combine yeast, sugar, 1 lb. of the flour and warm water in a large bowl. Let rest 1 hour.
Combine remaining flour with the salt, rub in the shortening, add to the yeast mixture to form a dough. Knead for 10 minutes, place on a floured table and let rise for 45 minutes covered with a clean cloth. Punch dough down, knead again for 2 minutes. Form into oblong shapes and place on a greased baking tray and allow to rise for 25 minutes. Bake in a preheated 375F Oven for 20-25 minutes.

ROTI FLAPS

1 lb. flour
3 tsps. baking powder
1 tsp. salt
2 Tbsps. oil
About 1 cup of water
Additional oil for cooking

Sift flour, baking powder and salt together. Add the 2 Tbsps. oil and enough water to make a stiff dough. Knead for 10 minutes, place in a well greased bowl, cover with a cloth and allow to rest for 1 hour. Knead again for 2 minutes, divide dough into 10-15 balls. Cover the balls with a cloth and rest for1 hour. Roll balls out on a lightly floured surface into thin large rounds the size of a dinner plate. Baste one side lightly with oil and place on a hot griddle or large frying pan, as the mixture cooks, little bumps will appear, brush flaps with oil and turn, pressing down on flaps as they cook. Do not overcook as flaps should remain pale and white. Place cooked flaps between a kitchen cloth while cooking remaining dough.

(Traditionally served as follows: Place 2-3 heaping Tbsps. of curry filling in centre, fold over one side, then opposite side. Repeat with top and bottom to form a totally enclosed parcel. Eat with your hands.)Curry fillings vary from all beef, all poultry, all shrimp or the aforesaid with potato added. They can be totally vegetarian as in all potato or any curried vegetable but peas and beans play a prominent part in this type of filling.
MAKES 4-6 flaps.

DHAL PURI FLAPS

1 recipe roti flaps above
½ lb. yellow split peas, soaked overnight
1 Tbsp. curry powder
1 tsp. ground cumin seed
1 onion minced fine
1 clove garlic minced fine
Salt to taste
1 tsp. oil

Heat the oil in a saucepan, fry curry, cumin, onion and garlic for a minute or so, add peas and enough water to just barely cover. Cook peas till soft and dry then mash or puree. Cool. Make roti flaps recipe, when forming into balls, flatten balls slightly, using thumb to make an indentation in the centre, add about a dessertspoon of split pea mixture and carefully pinch dough back into a ball shape. Proceed with roti flap recipe as directed above.

BUSS UP SHUTS *(Buss up Shuts so called because they resemble torn shirts are mainly used for dipping the bread into curry dishes with lots of gravy)*

Follow recipe for Roti Flaps.When cooked, tear into two or three pieces, return to griddle for a few seconds more.

ROTI FILLINGS: See recipes in index of individual curries to use as fillings.

Examples: Curry shrimp and potato   : Curry channa and potato
            : Curry chicken and potato : Curry beef and potato
            : Curry conch and potato   : Curry lamb and potato
OR: My favourite, follow recipe for curry chicken and potato substituting chicken livers and gizzards for the chicken.

Within The Brick Ovens

Preparing Dhal Puri roti flaps

Within The Brick Ovens

A special "Cove" breakfast for James, Paula and Kathy - Golden Flour Bakes served with scrambled eggs and flying fish

SPLIT PEA BARA BREAD

1 cup ground split pea flour
½ cup flour
3 tsps. baking powder
½ tsp. each salt, whole cumin and turmeric
1 garlic clove minced
1 small hot pepper minced
⅔ cup warm water

Combine split pea flour, flour, baking powder, salt, cumin, turmeric, garlic and hot pepper in a large bowl. Slowly add the water and mix thoroughly, adding more water or more flour as necessary to form a soft dough. Cover and allow to rest for 20-30 minutes. Form dough into 14 balls, flatten out the balls by hand to form a 3" to 4" diameter ¼" thick disk. Let rest for 10 minutes. Fry Baras in oil till golden and puffed, about 1 minute on each side.

BAKES (Various forms of bakes exist through out the islands with basically the same ingredients. In Trinidad they are famous for their Shark and Bake. In Jamaica they are known as Johnny Cakes. In Barbados they are associated with Salt Fish and Bakes. FLOATS from Trinidad are the yeast version of a Bake. Bakes may also be cooked on a hot griddle turning when lightly browned)

FLOUR BAKES

1 cup flour
2 tsps. baking powder
½ tsp. salt
1 tsp. sugar
2 Tbsps. shortening
5-6 Tbsps. water or more to make a soft dough

Combine flour, baking powder, salt and sugar. Cut in shortening with pastry blender and add water to make a soft dough. Knead 1 minute and rest at least 20 minutes. Pinch off balls and shape into flat rounds about ½" thick. Fry in hot oil till golden on both sides.

I serve these, split open, filled with salt fish bul jol as a snack or breakfast meal.

FLOATS *(A Trinidad bake using yeast)*

2 tsps. of dry yeast
Warm water
1 lb. flour
1½ tsps. salt
½ cup shortening

Dissolve yeast in a little warm water and rest for 5 minutes. Mix flour and salt, add shortening and cut in till mixture resembles fine crumbs. Add yeast along with additional water to make a soft dough. Knead till smooth. Place in a greased bowl, cover with a cloth and allow to rise for 2 hours or till doubled in size. Break off pieces and shape into egg sized balls. Allow to rise again for 20 minutes. Flatten out to ¼" thick bakes and deep fat fry in oil. *(Traditionally served with Accra a yeast raised salt fish fritter - see index)*

JOHNNY CAKES/BAKES

Follow recipe for FLOUR BAKES reducing the shortening to ¼ cup and increasing the baking powder to 2½ tsps. Bake on a greased griddle or in a preheated 425F Oven for 15-20 minutes.

CASSAVA BREAD

Bitter cassava
Salt to taste

Peel, wash and grate cassava finely. Wring out cassava in a cheese cloth to extract as much liquid as possible. Place cassava on a tray in the sun to dry for 30 minutes. Pound cassava, sift and mix with salt. Heat a griddle pan and a metal hoop the size of the bread to be made. Place cassava mixture in the ring to less than ¼" thick. Cook over medium heat till just beginning to set. Remove hoop, flatten cake with a spatula, pressing firmly and turn over to cook the other side. When cooked remove bread, stand upright and place in the sun to crisp.

Dumplings also known as spinners are a simple MUST for soups and stews in the Caribbean.

FLOUR DUMPLINGS

1 cup flour
2 tsps. baking powder
½ tsp. each salt and sugar
Pinch of mixed spice
1 Tbsp. butter
⅓-½ cup milk

Sift dry ingredients together, rub in butter, add milk and form into small balls. Rest in the fridge for 10 minutes. Drop on to hot soups or stews and cook covered for 15-20 minutes.

NUTMEG DUMPLINGS: Omit mixed spice and add ¼ tsp. freshly ground nutmeg.

HERBED DUMPLINGS: Add 1 Tbsp. of freshly chopped parsley or thyme or chives.

CORNMEAL DUMPLINGS

½ cup flour
1 cup cornmeal
¼ tsp. salt
3 tsps. baking powder
3 Tbsps. butter

Combine all dry ingredients, Rub in butter to crumb stage. Add a little water to make a stiff dough, form into small balls and cook in soups or stews for 30 minutes covered.

CASSAVA or FARINE DUMPLINGS

Substitute Cassava meal for corn meal in above recipe.

BEEF MARROW DUMPLINGS *(A little different but these are simply my favourite with a good beef stew. They remind me of the family fights we had as to whose turn it was to get the marrow from a steak bone - a family favourite!)*

½ cup mashed raw beef marrow from bones
1 cup soft bread crumbs
1 egg beaten
1 Tbsp. minced parsley
½ tsp. salt
Dash of black pepper

Combine all ingredients in a bowl, chill 30 minutes, shape into dumplings and rechill 30 minutes before adding to soups or stews. Cover pot and simmer 10-12 minutes.

Within The Brick Ovens

Carrenage, Inner Basin Barbados

Old Harbour Police - Barbados

Cutting canes

Sweety Vendors, are they becoming a thing of the Past?

What lovely memories we have of watching vendors with all their lovely home made candies.

These special folk would wake up early on a morning to get prime locations to sell their trays of goodies. In the market places, at the bus terminals, outside of the "film theatres", sitting patiently outside of schools, gathering places etc. Even songs have been written about them as they the vendors sing along the names of their hard labours to sell. Songs have been written about them and their "Calls" proclaiming what they are offering for sale.

The beauty of their sweets is in their using local produce to create these tasty morsels. Pages upon pages could be written about candy making in the Caribbean but set out here are a few samplers.

Guava Stew, I love this plain or over a bowl of Vanilla Ice Cream

Mangoes, papaw, pineapple may be similarly preserved.

GUAVA STEW

Ripe guavas
Granulated sugar
Piece of cinnamon stick
4 cloves
Fresh limejuice

Peel guavas and cut in half, removing seeds (Save for making jam or jelly). Weigh guavas and use the same weight in sugar. Place guavas in a large saucepan with water to just cover, add the sugar and spices with a little limejuice and cook till guavas are soft and a good thick syrup is formed. Bottle in hot sterilized jars.

GUAVA CHEESE

Ripe Guavas
Granulated sugar
Icing sugar for coating

Peel, remove seeds from guavas. Weigh guavas, add equal weight of sugar and the guavas to a saucepan. Bring to a boil then lower heat and simmer till mixture leaves the sides of the pan. Pour mixture into a greased and heavily sugared shallow pan and allow to set completely. When set, cut into squares and dredge in icing sugar till coated. Store in an airtight container.

MANGO CHEESE

Follow recipe for GUAVA CHEESE using ¾ cup of sugar plus 1 tsp. fresh limejuice to each cup of mango pulp.

MANGO PRESERVES

8 cups firm ripe mango flesh- cut in thick slices or cubes
½ cup lime juice
5 cups sugar
2" piece fresh ginger, sliced paper thin

Bring lime juice, sugar and ginger to a boil, cook stirring occasionally till slightly thickened, add mango and continue cooking until mango is glazed and mixture thick. Place in hot sterilized jars, seal and place in large saucepan of boiling water for 5 minutes. Cool and store

LIME AND PAW PAW BALLS

1 green paw paw, (measure after peeling, deseeding and grating)
1 cup granulated sugar per each cup measured paw paw - plus additional for coating
¼ cup water per each cup measured paw paw - plus additional for preparing the fruit
½ tsp. fresh limejuice to each cup of paw paw and a touch of grated lime rind
Green food colouring

Cover the paw paw in a saucepan with water, bring to a boil. Strain the water off, add fresh water and return to the boil. Strain paw paw once more and wring out the paw paw to remove as much liquid as possible. Make a thick syrup of the water, sugar proportioned to each cup of previously measured fruit. Add proportion of limejuice and a bit of rind, return the fruit to the pan and cook till mixture begins to harden. Add a little green colouring and remove from the heat. Cool slightly, form into small balls and roll in additional granulated sugar. Store in airtight containers when cool.

Sugar & Spice

TAMARIND BALLS

2 lbs. whole tamarinds
1 lb. sugar
1 Tbsp. limejuice
Dash of black pepper
Additional white sugar for coating
Shell the tamarinds, remove fibres and scrape off the pulp from the seeds. Add the sugar, limejuice and black pepper to the pulp and mix. Form into balls and coat with sugar.

KISSES/SOUPIES/MERRINGUES

2 ozs. castor sugar per every egg white
Beat egg white till stiff and dry, sprinkle with half the sugar and beat till glossy. Sift remaining sugar over and gently fold in. Place mixture by mounds or pipe on to a lightly greased baking sheet and place in a preheated 100F. for 5-6 hours. Store in airtight tin.

SHADDOCK RIND

1 shaddock
¾ cup of water
1½ lbs. of sugar - plus additional for coating
Very lightly grate the peel off a shaddock, cut into 1½" strips and soak in water to cover changing the water from time to time for 12 hours. Boil the rind in clean water till soft, discard this water, ring out the water from the rind. Place the sugar and the ¾ cup of water in a heavy saucepan and cook without stirring till a syrup is formed, drop the rind in the syrup and cook stirring from time to time till the syrup is absorbed. Remove from pan, roll in granulated sugar and dry in the sun.

SUGAR CAKES OR COCONUT ICE

½ lb. grated coconut
¼ pint of water
¾ lb. of sugar
Place sugar and water in a heavy saucepan, heat slowly to dissolve the sugar, add coconut and simmer till mixture thickens. Drop by spoonfulls on to waxed paper and cool. Food colouring is often added. Spices such as a pinch of cinnamon or nutmeg may also be added.

TOOLOOMS/ TULOONS/ TOOLUMS

1 lb. molasses
2 heaping Tbsps. brown sugar
2 Tbsps. dry ginger
1 coconut grated
Boil molasses, sugar and ginger until syrup spins a thread when dropped from a spoon. Add the coconut and cook till mixture thickens. Place by soup spoonfulls on a piece of wax paper and allow to cool. Store in airtight container.

RUM BALLS

1 cup chocolate chips, melted
⅓ cup rum
3 Tbsps. light corn syrup
2 ½ cups vanilla cookie crumbs
½ cup icing sugar
Granulated sugar for rolling balls in
Mix all ingredients except granulated sugar, shape into small balls and roll in granulated sugar. Store in an airtight container. Keep for three days before use to mature flavours.

Sugar & Spice

A tray of Caribbean sweets, tamarind balls, sugar cakes, toolooms and merringues

Sugar & Spice

An assortment of Fudges

Sugar & Spice

ALL FUDGES (*Use a candy thermometer for best results*) Once the butter is added, remove from heat and beat with electric beaters till glossy. Pour into a shallow well-greased pan and allow to set. Cut into squares while barely warm and allow to cool completely. Store in an airtight container.

AUNTY THELMA'S CHOCOLATE FUDGE (*Weird recipe but it works*)

4 cups sugar
1½ cups evaporated milk
4 Tbsps. cocoa powder
½ tsp. salt
½ cup butter
1 cup flour - **Yes flour!**
1 tsp. vanilla
Pinch of baking powder
Boil sugar, milk, cocoa and salt to hardball stage. Remove from heat, add flour, butter, baking powder and vanilla. Continue as above.

PINEAPPLE FUDGE

1 cup grated fresh pineapple
1 cup sugar
1 Tbsp. butter
Bring pineapple and sugar to a boil in a medium saucepan. Boil to hardball stage, stirring. Remove from heat, add butter, continue as above.

LIME FUDGE

1 lb. granulated sugar
2 cups milk
Grated rind and juice from 2 limes
1 Tbsp. butter
Combine sugar, milk in a saucepan, bring to a boil, boil till very thick and hardball stage is reached. Add butter, lime rind and limejuice. Continue as above.

VANILLA FUDGE (*Dried fruit or nuts may be added after the beating stage*)

1 lb. white sugar dissolved in ¼ cup water
1 tin of condensed milk
2 tsps. vanilla
2 Tbsps. butter
Combine sugar and milk in a large saucepan , bring mixture to a boil and cook to soft ball stage stirring all the time. Add butter and vanilla. Continue as above.

BANANA FUDGE

1 lb. granulated sugar
2 cups milk
2 large ripe bananas mashed
1 Tbsp. butter
1 tsp. fresh limejuice
Combine sugar, milk and bananas in a saucepan, bring to a boil, boil till very thick. Add butter and lime juice and continue as above.

Sugar & Spice

ORANGE FUDGE
2 ½ cups granulated sugar
½ cup milk
2 Tbsps. each of orange juice and orange rind
½ cup butter
Bring all ingredients except butter to a boil and cook to hardball stage. Cool slightly, then beat in the butter till creamy. Pour into well greased shallow baking pan. Cool completely and cut into squares.

BITTER SWEET CHEWS
½ lb. butter
¾ lb. granulated sugar
30 blanched cashew nuts
2 tsps. Angostura bitters
½ lb. milk chocolate
Melt the butter and sugar in a heavy saucepan over low heat stirring till sugar is dissolved. When sugar is dissolved and mixture boils, cook a further 2 minutes stirring. Remove from the heat, add bitters and nuts and pour into a greased flat 8" dish. Sprinkle the mixture with grated chocolate and let cool. When almost set, cut into squares and cool completely. Store in airtight containers.

GINGER CANDY
1 cup fresh peeled ginger, cut across the grain into slices
Water to just cover ginger
½ cup granulated sugar - plus additional for coating
¼ cup water
Cover ginger with water and boil for 5 minutes. In a heavy saucepan heat the ¼ cup water and the ½ cup of sugar and cook over low heat till a syrup is formed, add the ginger and continue cooking till syrup is absorbed, stirring from time to time to avoid burning. Remove ginger and place on a rack to dry for 1 hour. Roll in the additional granulated sugar and leave till sugar crystallizes. Store in airtight container.

PAW PAW CANDIED
1 young very firm but still green paw paw
1 lb. of sugar
2 cups water
1 tsp. butter per each pound of cooked pawpaw
Lime or orange rind
Make a few slashes in paw paw skin and leave to bleed. Place in boiling water and cook till just barely tender. Cut, remove seeds and cut into small pieces. Measure paw paw and add remainder of ingredients accordingly. Simmer till paw paw is clear and little syrup remains. Place on a piece of waxed paper to dry. Store in airtight containers.

PEANUT BRITTLE
2 cups sugar
1 cup chopped cooked nuts
Dash of salt
Melt sugar in a heavy saucepan till it caramelizes slightly and becomes a thin syrup. Add salt and nuts, place mixture in well greased pan and break into pieces when almost cool. COOL COMPLETELY and store in an airtight container.

Trinidad - Mountains & river

Dressing Her Up

Typical Bahamian boats - Bahamas

Guyana Docks

Dressing Her Up

A must in every Caribbean home - A "Lazy Susan" laden with lots of necessities

To me, a "Lazy Susan" on a table to accompany every meal is a must in every Caribbean home. Filled with our numerous chutneys, pepper jellies and the most important item, our famous HOT SAUCES. Add our tropical fruit Jams and Jellies for breakfast and lo and behold everything is available in one place.

West Indians like to 'dress up' everything and no matter how much hot pepper we use in our food preparation there is always a need to add just that little touch more.

Dressing Her Up

Guava Jelly, Passion Fruit jelly and Sorrel jam

Dressing Her Up

GUAVA JELLY

24 guavas
Water
Sugar
Juice of 1 lime
3 whole cloves
Small piece cinnamon stick
Wash guavas and quarter. Place in large saucepan with limejuice, cloves and cinnamon, barely cover with water, bring to a boil and cook till guavas are very soft. Cool,(use guavas for stew removing seeds) measure remaining liquid, add same amount of sugar, bring to a boil and cook to jelly stage. Place jelly in a cheesecloth bag and allow to seep through into jars for that clear look.

PASSION FRUIT JELLY

3 cups fresh passion fruit juice, reserving about ¼ cup seeds
7½ cups granulated sugar
1 cup water
Dash of ground ginger
1x6oz. bottle liquid pectin
Place passion fruit, sugar, water and ginger in a large heavy saucepan. Boil 5-8 minutes. Stir in liquid pectin and continue boiling 2-3 minutes longer. Bottle and seal in hot sterilized jars.

SORREL JAM

1 lb. of sorrel fruit, seeds removed, chopped fine
1 lb. granulated sugar
Small piece each of cinnamon bark, dried orange peel and a few whole cloves
Place sorrel in a large saucepan with just enough water to barely cover. Boil till sorrel is tender. Remove from heat, measure sorrel and liquid, return to the pan. To each cup of sorrel add 1 cup sugar with the cinnamon and orange peel. Bring to a boil, cook to soft ball stage. Remove cinnamon and peel, place in sterilized jars leaving open till cooled. Cover and store.

BARBADOS CHERRY JAM

4 cups very ripe Barbados cherries
Small piece of cinnamon
1 tsp. fresh limejuice
1 cup water
Granulated sugar
Boil, cherries and water till soft, cool, remove seeds, measure and return to saucepan adding ¾ cup sugar to each cup of pulp. Add cinnamon stick and limejuice bring to a boil and cook to soft ball stage. Remove cinnamon and pour into hot sterilized jars. Seal and cool.

TAMARIND JAM

1½ cups shelled tamarinds
5 cups boiling water
1 cup granulated sugar to every cup of tamarind pulp
Small piece of cinnamon
Pour boiling water over tamarinds. Cool, strain and measure liquid. Add sugar accordingly with cinnamon stick, bring to a boil and cook to soft ball stage. Place in hot sterilized jars, seal and cool.

In Trinidad pieces of chopped chadon bene are often added with a variety of yellow, red hot peppers and the garlic volume is greatly increased. Small chunks of green but firm papaw may also be added.

PEPPER SAUCE *(Barbados version)*

6 hot peppers, deseeded and minced
1 large onion minced
1 large garlic clove minced
1 Tbsp. dry mustard
¼ cup white vinegar
1 Tbsp. oil
½ tsp. salt

Combine all ingredients in a saucepan, bring to a boil, lower heat and simmer 15 minutes, store in clean sterilized jars.

PEPPER SAUCE *(Windward island version)*

8 hot red peppers washed and deseeded
1 large onion chopped
2 cloves garlic minced
1 tsp. salt
3 tsps. dry mustard
1 cup white vinegar
1 Tbsp. oil
Pinch tumeric or saffron powder
4 whole cloves

Place all the ingredients in a saucepan, boil for 20 minutes. Puree and pack into sterilized jars.

PEPPER WINE

Bird peppers (tiny little red elongated peppers) or wiri wiri (small round peppers)
Sherry or rum

Wash bird peppers and prick them carefully with a pin, place in sterilized jars and cover with either rum or sherry. Cover and store for a few weeks before use.

This recipe was given to me by a Jamaican friend "Pata" Read. I use is to serve with many pork or chicken dishes both as an accompaniment and to mix up with other ingredients to create glazes.

PEPPER JELLY

¼ cup finely chopped red and green hot peppers
½ cup finely chopped sweet red and green sweet peppers
6½ cups granulated sugar
1½ cups cider vinegar
6oz. bottle of liquid pectin

Mix peppers with sugar and vinegar. Bring to a boil and boil at a full roll for 5 minutes. Stir in pectin and continue to boil 2 minutes longer. Remove from heat, cool slightly and bottle in hot sterilized jars. Seal.

FRESH HOT PEPPER CONDIMENT

Dice hot seeded peppers into really tiny pieces. Add salt and lime juice. Let sit overnight. Serve with any meal.

Dressing Her Up

Peppersauces and Pepperjelly

Dressing Her Up

Variety of Chutneys and Chows

Dressing Her Up

CHUTNEYS (*chutneys form an integral part of our Caribbean cuisine. Tables are normally set with a chutney or two, a pepper sauce, a pepper jelly and some form of a pickle. Most chutney flavours are enhanced if you let them sit for 1 month after making. FRESH CHUTNEYS should be kept refrigerated and eaten within a few days*)

FRESH MANGO CHUTNEY

2 firm but full green mangoes, peeled and grated
2 garlic cloves minced
1 tsp. salt
½ small hot pepper minced
1 Tbsp. olive oil
1 chadon bene leaf minced
Combine all ingredients in blender or food processor. Store in covered jar refrigerated and use within a few days.

MANGO or TAMARIND ACHAR

Green full mangoes or tamarind pulp
Salt, vinegar, hot pepper, mustard seed, cumin seed, mustard oil
Mince mangoes or tamarind with a little salt and vinegar. Heat a bit of oil in a heavy saucepan, cook mustard seeds and cumin seeds till just fragrant, add mango or tamarind and cook till soft. Pour into jars and refrigerate.

PRESERVED MANGO CHUTNEY

25 green, full mangoes, peeled and diced
1 lb. currants
½ lb. raisins
¼ lb. fresh ginger
¼ lb. garlic
¼ lb. salt
2 hot peppers minced
5 lbs. sugar
3 x 26 oz. bottles of vinegar
Grind mangoes, ginger and garlic together, place in a stainless steel bowl with one bottle of vinegar and leave overnight. Place mixture in large saucepan, add remaining ingredients, bring to a boil and lower heat, cook stirring from time to time till thick and syrupy, about 2½ hours. Pour into hot sterilized jars and seal.

TAMARIND CHUTNEY

¼ lb. shelled tamarind pods
1¼ cups hot water
1 cup sugar
1 tsp. each garam masala, ground roasted cumin seeds and salt
½ tsp. hot pepper minced
1 cup raisins
Soak the tamarind in the hot water, cool and remove seeds. Place mixture in a heavy saucepan with the sugar, garam masala, cumin, hot pepper and salt, bring to a boil, reduce heat and simmer 10 minutes. Add raisins, bring back to a boil and cook 2-3 minutes longer. Cool and store in sterilized airtight jars.

Dressing Her Up

GOLDEN APPLE CHUTNEY
2 lbs. peeled, deseeded and chopped golden apples
¼ lb. chopped onions
2 cups brown sugar
1 Tbsp. salt
1 tsp. fresh grated ginger
½ tsp. ground cloves
1 cup white vinegar
Combine all ingredients in a large saucepan, bring to a boil, reduce heat and cook stirring till thick and syrupy. Seal in hot sterilized jars.

LIME CHUTNEY
12 limes, sliced
1¼ lbs. granulated sugar
1 cup cider vinegar
Pinch of salt
3 Tbsps. water
2" stick of cinnamon bark
1 tsp. whole allspice
2 ozs. fresh peeled grated ginger
4 cloves
Small piece hot pepper minced
Remove seeds from limes. Place the sugar, vinegar, salt, water, ginger and the spices. Boil at full for 5 minutes. Add limes, hot pepper and continue cooking at a full boil for 3 minutes longer. Place limes in sterilized jars, top with remaining syrup. Seal.

Two types of CHOW CHOW exist, the spicy mustard pickle always found on tables in days of old and the quick mango version which we consumed by the handful as children, preferably eating it while up the mango tree.

CHOW CHOW *(mustard pickle)*

1 cucumber, peeled and coarsely chopped	5 cups wine vinegar
10 small onions, coarsely chopped	½ lb. sugar
3 green tomatoes, coarsely chopped	2 Tbsps. cornstarch
12 string beans, cut in half	1 tsp. turmeric
1 cauliflower separated into flowerets	2 Tbsps. dry mustard
1 hot pepper, minced	1 tsp. curry powder
2 Tbsps salt	

Place all the vegetables in a stainless steel basin, dissolve the salt in 3 cups of water and pour over the vegetables, cover and leave overnight. Next day, drain the vegetables and place in large saucepan along with 1 cup of water, 2 Tbsps. of the vinegar and bring to a boil, lower heat and continue cooking at a simmer for 5 minutes. Meanwhile combine the cornstarch with the sugar, turmeric, mustard and curry. Use a little of the remaining vinegar to make a smooth paste, mix in all the vinegar. Add a few tablespoons of the vegetable liquid to the cornstarch and stir in then stir in the cornstarch into the vegetables, simmer 2 minutes longer. Place in hot sterilized jars and seal.

CHOW CHOW
Full but green mangoes, salt and pepper to taste, piece of hot pepper minced, vinegar. Peel and slice the mangoes, sprinkle with salt and pepper, toss with the hot pepper and vinegar.

Cariacou - Paradise island

Village in Dominica

Cheers

Bajan Rum shops

Cheers

My daughters, Laura and Judy with the traditional sundown RUM COCKTAIL

The Caribbean produces the finest RUM in the world with each island claiming that theirs is the best. With Rum as a base many exotic drinks are created by our barmen, but we also have our traditional non alcoholic drinks such as Mawby, Sorrel and numerous fruit drinks to quench the thirst.

I am glad to see more and more fresh juice stalls springing up and successfully competing with our "snow cone"(shaved ice placed in a cone with a heavy thick syrup poured over and in most cases topped with condensed milk) vendors and our coconut water vendors.

Cheers

An original Rum Punch, topped with bitters and freshly grated nutmeg

Cheers

RUM PUNCH *(This is a genuine recipe along with its little jingle, many recipes have been created and called a RUM PUNCH but nothing is better than the true original old time version)*

Ye Old RECIPE: TRANSALATION:

1 of sour   1 cup fresh limejuice
2 of sweet   2 cups sugar syrup - *s ee recipe in inde*x
3 of strong   3 cups rum
4 of weak   4 cups water

Mix all together and stir till well combined. Serve over lots of crushed ice, add a few dabs of Angostura bitters and sprinkle with freshly grated nutmeg before serving. SERVES 8.

PLANTER'S PUNCH

2 Tbsps. limejuice
2 Tbsps. simple syrup - *see recipe in index*
¼ cup rum
¼ cup orange juice
Dash of Angostura bitters
Crushed ice
Combine all ingredients and shake, pour over crushed ice. SERVES 2.

PIRATE'S PUNCH

2 ozs. rum
1 oz. vermouth
Dash of Angostura bitters
½ cup crushed ice
Place all ingredients in cocktail shaker and shake vigorously. SERVES 1.

PINA COLADA

4 oz. pineapple juice
2 ozs. sweet coconut cream
2 ozs. rum
½ cup crushed ice
Place all ingredients in a blender. Blend a few seconds, pour into glass and decorate with a piece of pineapple and a cherry. SERVES 1.

BLUE MOUNTAIN COCKTAIL

1½ ozs. rum
¾ oz. vodka
¾ oz. Tia Maria or any coffee liqueur
2 Tbsps. orange juice
1 Tbsp. limejuice
Crushed ice.
Combine all ingredients in a cocktail shaker and shake vigorously. SERVES 1.

RUM SOUR *(This one is for Lady Lewis)*

In a cocktail shaker, combine:
2 ozs. white rum, 1oz. lime syrup - *recipe follows* with 1 cup of crushed ice. Shake vigorously, pour into a glass. Serve topped with a dash of Angostura bitters. SERVES 1.

LIME SYRUP

Combine ¼ cup fresh limejuice with ½ cup simple syrup- **see index.** Shake well, store in the refrigerator. A handy recipe, use for making fresh limejuice by combining 1½ ozs. of mixture with water and ice or similarly lime squash by using soda instead of water.

As children we could always tell when it was 6 o'clock in the evening for precisely at this hour the parents would take out the old silver cocktail shaker and shake, a practice they still do up to today. Every child then grandchild and finally great grandchild had to learn to mix these in the early. Now the thing to do is to fix the first round , adding all the ingredients and hand the shaker over to one of your guests to shake- give as many guests a turn. THE BEST COCKTAIL SHAKER IS THE PERSON WHO OBTAINS THE FROTHIEST HEAD!

DAD'S RUM COCKTAIL

4 Cocktail shaker tops of rum
1 Cocktail shaker top of water or a pass through of water (this means let the tap water run and pass the shaker slowly under it)
3-4 dashes Angostura bitters
Lots of crushed ice
Place all ingredients in cocktail shaker, shake vigorously. SERVES 4.

SWEET RUM COCKTAIL

4 cocktail shaker tops of rum
1 cocktail shaker top of water
3-4 dashes Angostura bitters
½ Cocktail shaker top of sugar syrup - *see recipe in index*
½ cup crushed ice
Small piece lime peel
Combine all ingredients in a Cocktail shaker and shake away! SERVES 4.

This is a Bay House favourite usually consumed before the gigantic lunch is served, also known as pink gin.

GIN COCKTAIL

4 ozs. gin
3-4 dashes Angostura bitters
1 tsp. sugar
Small piece lime peel
½ cup crushed ice.
Place all ingredients in cocktail shaker and shake vigorously. SERVES 3.

I have often served this at the end of a late breakfast jokingly telling my guests that I'm sure their mothers told them they had to drink a glass of milk with their morning meal.

WHITE LADY *(Another Bay House Special or morning drink)*

1 large tin of evaporated milk (Save tin for measuring the rum)
1 tin of condensed milk
1 (evaporated tin measure) of rum
Angostura bitters and freshly grated nutmeg to garnish
Crushed ice
Combine liquid ingredients, stirring till evaporated milk is mixed in. Chill. Serve over lots of crushed ice and top with a few dashes of bitters and freshly grated nutmeg. SERVES 6.

Cheers

Mum and Dad, Gordon & Dickie Parkinson shaking the 'good ole' rum cocktail on their gallery.
So many "Bajans", West Indians and visitors to our island have shared these cocktails with them

Cheers

Orange Daiquiri

I am giving the basic recipe for to this, you can add any tropical fruit in season to make daiquiri.

DAIQUIRI BASIC RECIPE

3 ozs. rum
½ oz. lime juice
2 ozs. simple syrup - *see index*
½ cup crushed ice
Place ingredients along with selected fruit in a blender and mix till frosted.
Adjust with additional syrup according to the tartness of the fruit used.

BANANA: Add ½ small banana and 1 oz. Banana liqueur.

COCONUT: Add ½ cup coconut cream and 1 oz. coconut liqueur.

LIME: Increase limejuice to 2 Tbsps. Add 1 oz. orange liqueur.

MANGO: Add ½ cup chopped ripe mango and 1 oz. orange liqueur.

ORANGE: Add ½ cup segmented fresh sweet orange pieces and 1 oz. orange liqueur.

PAPAW: Add ½ cup peeled, deseeded cubes of paw paw and 1 oz. orange liqueur.

PASSION FRUIT: Use pulp from 1 fruit and add 1 oz. orange liqueur.

PINEAPPLE: Add ½ cup fresh pineapple chunks with 1 oz. orange liqueur.

SOUR SOP: Add 1 cup sour sop pulp with 1 oz. orange liqueur.

TAMARIND: Add 2 Tbsps. tamarind puree plus 2 oz. orange liqueur.

TROPICAL FRUIT: Add 1 cup frozen tropical mixed fruit with 1 oz. orange liqueur.

TO MAKE FROZEN DAIQUIRIS - Freeze mixture then place in a blender to mix.

Cheers

Ponche Crema is a Christmas tradition throughout the islands, because of its high rum content it will keep for a few days in its uncooked version or longer in its cooked version but must be properly refrigerated. Bottles are made and kept in the refrigerator for instant offerings.

PONCHE CREMA 1

6 eggs
1 tin condensed milk
1 cup rum
Few drops each vanilla and lime juice
Angostura bitters and freshly grated nutmeg for garnish.

Combine eggs, condensed milk, rum, vanilla and limejuice in a blender, mix till smooth. Chill. Serve over lots of crushed ice, garnish with a few drops Angostura and a dash of grated nutmeg.

PONCHE CREMA 2

6 eggs   3 cups rum
4 cups milk   6 Tbsps. cornstarch
1 cup sugar   Vanilla essence to taste

Combine the cornstarch with a little milk to dissolve, mix in with the remaining milk and bring to a boil stirring. Meanwhile beat eggs till frothy, slowly add hot milk to egg mixture, return to the stove, reduce heat, stir till slightly thickened. Do not allow to boil. Add rum and vanilla, cool and chill. Serve garnished with bitters and freshly grated nutmeg.

Bottlefuls are made for Christmas, when sorrel is plentiful. Nowadays dried sorrel is available through out the year.

SORREL

3 cups, seeded sorrel
6 cups water
½" square piece of ginger
Small piece dried orange peel
6 cloves
2 cups sugar

Place sorrel in a jar with bruised ginger, peel and cloves. Pour boiling water over and leave covered overnight. Strain, add sugar stirring till dissolved. Cover, leave for one more day. Chill.

EGG NOG or EGG FLIP

4 ozs. Rum
½ cup evaporated milk
1 egg. lightly beaten
1 tsp. sugar
½ cup crushed ice
Dash of Angostura biters
Grated fresh nutmeg to garnish

Place all ingredients except bitters and nutmeg in cocktail shaker or blender and shake vigorously. Serve garnished with bitters and topped with nutmeg.

CHILDREN'S EGG NOG or FLIP

Follow recipe as above omitting the rum.
My parents used to serve these to us as children, we felt very grown up drinking an adult drink, yet there was no alcohol, it also guaranteed that we were eating eggs!

Cheers

Christmas drinks of red Sorrel and white Ponche Crema

Coconut Punch

Cheers

CORN n OIL *(Typically Barbadian)*
½ oz. falernum - *recipe follows*
1 oz. rum
Combine ingredients and serve.

FALERNUM *(used in CORN n OIl and to sweeten and flavour many Caribbean drinks. Originated in Barbados by supposedly a Henry Parkinson, a pharmacists - one of my ancestors)*
2 lbs. granulated sugar
10 cups water
⅓ cup fresh limejuice
6 drops almond essence
2½ cups white rum
Heat sugar with half the water stirring to dissolve, remove from heat, add remaining ingredients and stir well. Cool and bottle.

COCONUT PUNCH - *see index for recipe.*
3 cups homemade coconut milk
1 tin condensed milk
2 cups rum
Dash of almond essence
2 dashes vanilla essence
Grated nutmeg
Combine all ingredients in a large pitcher. Chill, serve over crushed ice. SERVES 6.

COCONUT RUM
3 ozs. coconut milk
½ oz. falernum
2½ ozs. rum
½ cup crushed ice
Combine all ingredients in a shaker, shake vigorously, serve in coconut shells. SERVES 2.

CARIBBEAN COFFEE
Strong black coffee
1 oz. each Tia Maria and rum
Lightly whipped cream
Irish Coffee mugs
Place Tia Maria and rum in an Irish coffee glass. Pour over boiling coffee and gently pour the cream over this. *A little cinnamon may be sprinkled over the whipped cream.*

Usually served towards the end of a wedding to assist in the sobering up process before going home. Small 2-3 oz. cups are used for serving. Can be made well in advance and frozen.
ICED COFFEE
1 cup evaporated milk
¼ cup condensed milk
2 cups extra strong coffee made with milk or 5-6 heaping tsps. instant coffee dissolved in 2 cups milk. Combine all ingredients, chill. SERVES 6.

Cheers

GINGER BEER

1 gallon of boiling water
2 ozs. fresh ginger pounded or finely grated
Juice and rind from 2 limes
1 tsp. yeast
1½ lb. sugar

Pour boiling water over ginger and juice and rind of limes, stir and allow to steep till lukewarm. Dissolve yeast in a little warm water and stir into the ginger mixture. Leave for 6-8 hours, covered in plastic wrap. Sweeten with the sugar and bottle and chill.

MAWBY

Large piece of mawby bark
Small piece dried orange peel
½" piece cinnamon stick
4 cloves
1 blade of mace
12 cups water
2 cups sugar

Boil the mawby bark along with the orange peel, cinnamon, cloves and mace with 1 cup of water for 5 minutes at a rolling boil. Cool, strain and add remaining water and sugar, stir till sugar is dissolved. Bottle and leave for 3 days. Chill.

SEA MOSS DRINK

½ lb. sea moss
Limejuice
Stick of cinnamon and a dash of grated fresh nutmeg
4 cups water
Vanilla essence
Sugar to sweeten

Wash sea moss in limejuice and soak overnight. Strain and discard the water. Place in a large saucepan with 4 cups fresh water, stick of cinnamon and nutmeg and cook till soft. Strain while warm, add essence to taste and sweeten with sugar. Chill.

QUICK PEANUT PUNCH

1 oz. creamy peanut butter
1 cup milk
1-2 tsps. sugar
Lots of crushed ice

Mix all ingredients in a blender till smooth and frothy. SERVES 1.

TROPICAL PUNCH

1 cup fresh orange juice
1 cup fresh grapefruit juice
1 cup pineapple juice
½ cup fresh lime juice
1 cup water
½ cup simple syrup - *see recipe in index*
2 bottles ginger ale or sprite

Mix all ingredients together. Serve immediately with lots of ice.

Cheers

Top - Sea Moss, Middle - Mawby, Bottom - Ginger Beer

Cheers

Tart and thirst quenching fresh Tamarind Water

Cheers

MANGO SMOOTHIE
Combine in a blender 2 cups mango pulp with 1 cup evaporated milk, sugar to taste and a few drops of lime juice. Serve over crushed ice.

SHANDY
1 bottle of beer
1 bottle of ginger beer (Preferably home made - *see recipe in index*)
Combine ingredients in a jug, serve over ice.

TAMARIND WATER
1 lb. shelled tamarinds
4 cups boiling water
2 cups sugar or add more to taste
Soak tamarinds in boiling water for 1-2 hours. Scrape off pulp, sweeten and swizzle to combine and dissolve sugar. Chill, serve with lots of ice.

SOURSOP PUNCH
1 soursop
4 cups cold water
Strip of lime peel
Condensed milk to sweeten
Mash soursop in a bowl, slowly add half the water and mash with your fingers to extract as much pulp as possible. Strain, add remaining water and sweeten to taste with the condensed milk. Chill, serve with lots of ice.

PASSION FRUIT DRINK
Scoop out seeds from passion fruit, mix with water and sugar to taste. Strain and chill.

GUAVA DRINK
1 lb. ripe guavas
1 cup sugar
4 cups water
Juice from ½ a lime
Peel guavas and remove all the seeds. Place in a blender with the remaining ingredients. Chill and serve over ice.

GOLDEN APPLE DRINK
8 peeled seeded golden apples
6 cups water
Juice from 1 lime
Sugar to sweeten
Combine all ingredients in a blender, chill, serve over ice.

SUGAR APPLE DRINK
4 sugar apples
¼ cup condensed milk
1 cup water
Combine all ingredients well. Strain, serve over ice cubes.

This is a family favourite when entertaining visitors, it is not only economical but makes such a beautiful show at night. It is my Father's specialty.

POOR MAN'S LIQUEUR

6 ozs. rum
4 dessert spoonfuls of sugar
Peel of 1 lime cut in one continuous piece
Place lime peel and sugar in a heatproof small dish with the rum. Using a spoon with a long handle, scoop up some rum, heat it gently, ignite and return flames to dish. Stir to dissolve the sugar and burn the peel. Put out the flames after 2-3 minutes and serve hot in liqueur glasses.

COFFEE LIQUEUR

4 cups water
3 cups sugar
½ cup instant coffee granules
3 tsps. vanilla
2 ½ cups white rum or vodka
1 ½ tsps. glycerine
Bring water to a boil with the sugar and coffee, lower heat and simmer for 1 hour. Add remaining ingredients and bottle, store in a dark place for one month before use.

Jamaica does a gorgeous Tangerine liqueur using gin and well worth a try.

TANGERINE LIQUEUR

18 ripe tangerines (peeled, reserve peel - squeeze juice)
8 cups gin
3 lbs. granulated sugar
Juice from the tangerines plus cold water to make up 4 cups
Wash the peels well and soak in the gin for 2 days. Strain. Boil juice/water with the sugar for 10 minutes, stirring to dissolve the sugar. Strain. Combine the vodka mixture and the syrup mixture and bottle. Leave for one month before using.

Sorrel Liqueur is traditionally made for the Christmas season, this recipe comes from Grenada.

SORREL LIQUEUR

3 lbs. sorrel, cleaned and deseeded
26 oz. bottle of rum
3 lbs. granulated sugar
3 tsps. Angostura bitters
1 piece fresh mace
Place all ingredients in a large glass jar. Cover and place in a dark cupboard for 1 month. Strain and bottle.

PASSION FRUIT LIQUEUR

⅓ cup passion fruit pulp or more to taste
1 cup boiling water
1 ½ cups sugar
1 ½ cups white rum
Pour boiling water over passion fruit pulp Allow to cool slightly. Add sugar and rum and place in a large glass jar. Cover and place in a dark cupboard for 1 month. Strain and bottle.

Cheers

Coffee Liqueur

Misc – Hints, Tips, Substitutes, References

Old Barbados Hilton and Engineer's pier

Miss Nurse's Old bath house on the west coast of Barbados

BASIC WHITE SAUCE

2 Tbsps. butter
2 Tbsps. flour
1 cup milk
Salt and pepper to taste
Melt butter in a saucepan, add flour and cook till incorporated stirring constantly. Slowly add milk whisking continuously. Cook stirring till thick.

VARIATIONS ON WHITE SAUCE

CHEESE: Add 1tsp. Worcestershire sauce, pinch of dry mustard and ½ cup grated cheddar cheese at the end.

CURRY: MILD - Add 1 tsp. curry powder with the butter before adding the flour.
: STRONG - Add 1 Tbsp. curry powder as above.

HERBED: Add 2 Tbsps, chopped chives and 3 Tbsps. chopped parsley at the end.

LIME: Add juice from ½ a lime or more to taste at the end.

NUTMEG: Add ¼ tsp. freshly grated nutmeg with the butter and flour.

STOCK SAUCE: Add 1 stock cube, either fish, chicken or beef with the milk

SIMPLE SYRUP

4 cups sugar
2 cups boiling water
Combine ingredients in a large bowl and stir till sugar is dissolved.

SPICY BATTER FOR FRYING FISH OR SHRIMP

1 cup flour
1 cup water
1 heaping tsp. baking powder
1 Tbsp. hot sauce
1 Tbsp. Caribbean seasoning - *see index for recipe*
Combine all ingredients and whisk till smooth.

BUTTERED CRUMBS *(to use as a topping for dishes)*

3 Tbsps. melted butter
¼ cup dry breadcrumbs
Combine all ingredients. Place over casserole dish, additionally you may sprinkle with herbs or cheese and top off with a little paprika powder.

CHEESEY CRUMBS
To buttered crumbs add ¼ cup grated parmesan cheese
HERBED CRUMBS
To above recipe add ¼ cup chopped fresh parsley or chives.

Misc - Hints, Tips, Substitutes, References

TRINIDAD SEASONINGS: Coarsely chop together the following:
1 large onion minced, 2 garlic cloves minced, 5 blades chive minced, 1 stalk celery minced, 2 Tbsps. vinegar, 2 Tbsps. rum, 1 Tbsp. Worcestershire sauce, piece of hot pepper minced. Store in an airtight container in the fridge.

BARBADOS SEASONINGS: Coarsely chop together the following:
1 bunch chives, small onion, 3 garlic cloves, 1 small hot pepper, 1 Tbsp fresh thyme, ½ tsp.fresh marjoram, ¼ tsp. ground cloves, 1 tsp. salt and 1 Tbsp. fresh limejuice. Store in airtight jar in refrigerator.

JAMAICA JERK SEASONINGS: Coarsely chop together the following:
1 large onion minced, 1 cup chives minced, 5 garlic cloves minced, 2 tsp. fresh thyme, 1 hot pepper minced, 3 tsps. salt, 2 tsps. sugar, 2 tsps. freshly ground pimento or Allspice, ¼ tsp. each fresh ground nutmeg and mace, ½ tsp. black pepper. Store in an airtight container in the fridge.

BAY SAUCE
1 onion chopped
Small piece hot pepper minced
Juice from 1 lime
¼ cup hot water
¼ cup red salted or normal butter
Combine all ingredients, use to pour over hot cooked breadfruit, or cooked okras, or cooked green bananas etc.

PICKLE
Use recipe for pickle in souce - **see index** to pour over cold cooked breadfruit, cooked conch, boiled cooked tripe, boiled green bananas etc.

COCONUT MILK AND CREAM
3 cups grated fresh coconut
1 cup boiling water
Pour boiling water over coconut, leave for one hour. Wring out through a cheesecloth extracting as much liquid as possible.
TO MAKE CREAM - refrigerate for a couple of hours and the cream will rise to the top.
TO MAKE MILK - use as is or the leftover liquid after removing the cream.
FOR USE IN DESSERTS - Use milk instead of the water.

COCONUT OIL
2 dry coconuts
½ cup water
Grate coconuts, mix with the water and blend in a food processor or blender. Ring out in a cheesecloth or muslin bag. Place liquid in a heavy saucepan and boil till liquid becomes oil. **Coconut oil is excellent in curries.**

TOASTED COCONUT
Place grated coconut on a tray, bake in a preheated 375F oven for 8-10 minutes, turning often. Use for decorating desserts or serve with curries.

Herbs used to make Caribbean "Seasonings"

Cassareep and ingredients for its preparation

CANDIED CITRUS

Thinly slice lime and oranges, leave whole or cut in halves. Coat thoroughly with granulated sugar on both sides, place on a sheet of waxed paper on a baking tray. Leave in the sun for 4-5 hours, turning from time to time. Use to decorate desserts.

BROWNING *(Home made browning or caramel food colouring is used extensively in Caribbean cooking. Make a jar full and store)*

2 cups sugar
1 Tbsp. oil
½ cup water.
In large HEAVY SAUCEPAN, heat oil and sugar till sugar dissolves and cook till sugar becomes a very dark brown colour but do not allow to burn. This takes about 8 minutes. Now, be very careful, remove from heat and slowly add water in a thin stream. Mixture will bubble up and splatter. When splattering stops, stir, cool and store.

CASSAREEP

4 lbs. cassava, peeled and finely grated
1 cup water
1 tsp. ground cinnamon
½ tsp. ground cloves
1 heaping Tbsp. brown sugar
Add water to grated cassava and stir well. Use several thicknesses of muslin or cheesecloth and squeeze and ring the cassava till all the liquid is extracted. Reserve the grated cassava to make farine or cassava meal - *see index*. Place the squeezed liquid in a saucepan together with the cinnamon, cloves and sugar. Bring to a boil, reduce heat and simmer slowly, stirring from time to time till thick and syrupy.
Use in Pepperpot.
Makes about 1 cup.

SHADOW BENE SAUCE *(for Shark & Bake)*

¼ cup minced Shadow Bene or fresh coriander
½ cup white wine vinegar or fresh lime juice
1 garlic clove minced
1 tsp. each corn oil and sugar
¼ of a hot pepper minced
Pinch of salt
Combine all ingredients in a jar and allow to stand for a few hours.

CARIBBEAN SPICED THOUSAND ISLAND DRESSING

½ cup tomato ketchup
1 tsp. chilli powder
1 tsp. Worcestershire Sauce
1 tsp. fresh limejuice
¼ cup mayonnaise
Whip all ingredients till smooth. Adjust flavours to suit with additional limejuice to taste. Add a bit of salt if needed.
Herbs such as parsley or finely grated onion may be added.

PREPARATION OF BANANA LEAVES FOR COOKING *(i.e Pastelles, Doucama and Conkies.*
Please note the leaves are not edible)
EITHER: Singe the leaves over an open flame ie the stove or outside fire till they soften then clean and cut into 8" squares.
OR: Cut into 8"squares, plunge in boiling water for a minute or so.
These freeze beautifully.
OR: Cut into 8" squares and place in a preheated hot oven for 5 minutes.

SEA GRAPE LEAVES
In some of the islands, sea grape leaves are used for wrapping foods. If using, either follow directions for banana leaves or singe in boiling water till just soft and pliable.

SPICY BATTER FOR FRYING FISH OR SHRIMP
1 cup flour
1 cup water
1 tsp. baking powder
1 Tbsp. hot sauce
1 Tbsp. Caribbean seasoning - *see index for recipe*
Combine all ingredients and whisk till smooth.

CHOCOLATE ICING
Combine 1 lb. icing sugar with ½ cup cocoa powder. Cream ½ cup butter adding sugar mixture slowly. Add 4 Tbsps. milk and 1½ tsps. vanilla whipping till combined. Enough to ice 1 cake.

COFFEE ICING
Cream ½ cup butter adding 1 lb. icing sugar slowly. Add 2 Tbsps. coffee dissolved in 4 Tbsps. milk.

ORANGE ICING
Cream ½ cup butter adding 1 lb. icing sugar slowly. Add 2 tsps. grated orange rind with 4 tbsps. orange juice.

LIME ICING
Cream ½ cup butter adding 1 lb. icing sugar slowly. Add 2 tsps. grated lime rind with 2 Tbsps. fresh lime juice mixed with 2 Tbsps. water.

Keeps for two to three weeks. Use a large tablespoon per serving to any fish, seafood poultry beef or lamb for a quick curry.
CURRY PASTE
¼ cup oil
4 onions coarsely chopped
8 garlic cloves minced
¼ cup oil
⅓ cup good curry powder
¼ cup whole cumin or geera seeds
Heat oil, fry onions and garlic 3-4 minutes, add curry powder and cumin seeds continue to fry 2-3 minutes, add ¼ cup water, fry stirring till water evaporates. Add another ¼ cup water and cook till a few minutes longer. Store refrigerated in covered container.

Diagram for folding banana leaves for pastelles

1. Place dough on flat leaf, flatten dough. Add meat misxture.

2. Fold leaf over to meet opposite side.

3. Double fold to secure.

4. Fold in both open sides.

5. Tie with soft string and knot.

Preparing Banana leaves for use in cooking

It is only fitting that I end the recipe chapters with sketches of the greatest game that unites us all in the West Iindies. Cricket glorious cricket!

We are very proud to be Bajans, Trinis, Guyanese, Vincentians, St. Lucians, Antiguans, Jamaican Domincans, etc etc until a game is on: then and only then are we WEST INDIANS as one!

A countryside cricket pavillion

The game of cricket in action

HINTS AND TIPS

BEEF/LAMB: Sprinkle tough beef or lamb with a pinch of baking soda to tenderize.

SHRIMP: Soak shrimp in 1cup water plus 1 tsp. baking soda for 2 minutes. Drain and rinse well. Removes sliminess and keeps shrimp tender.

POTATOES: When BBQing a simple meal, Microwave your potatoes till just cooked then immediately place them on the BBQ along with what you are BBQing. It crisps up the skins.

CITRUS FRUIT: Microwave whole oranges, limes, grapefruits for a few seconds before squeezing. It releases more juice.

WHITE SAUCE: To ensure a lump free white sauce, use a whisk and whisk constantly till sauce thickens.

GRAVY: When making gravy, use the pan the roast was cooked in, all the lovely roast seasonings are incorporated in the gravy plus it helps clean the pan of hard caked on bits.

GELATIN: In hot weather, add 1 tsp. white vinegar to gelatin salads. It helps to keep them firmer for a longer time.

MERINGUE: For a fluffier meringue, add ¼ tsp. vinegar for every three egg whites used and whip.

PIES: Brush tops of pies with vinegar and return to the oven for a few minutes for a nice sheen.

SALTY FOODS: Add sugar and lime juice to reduce saltiness.

HOT PEPPER FOODS: If too hot to eat, use limejuice and sugar to calm down the fire.

DRIED HERBS: Fry herbs a few seconds before adding remaining ingredients. It brings out more flavour.

CAULIFLOWER: Add 1-2 tsps. vinegar to the water you are cooking the cauliflower in, it keeps the flowerets whiter.

FRYING CHICKEN: Fry till barely brown, turn and fry again till barely brown. Cover pan, reduce heat to low and continue cooking chicken 5-8 minutes. Remove cover, increase heat and fry to recrisp skin and finish cooking. Covering the pan ensures not only that the chicken is cooked through but nice and moist.

ROASTING MEATS: Take the guess work out of perfect roasts, use a meat thermometer to ensure roast is cooked to personal preference.

ROASTS: Roasts can be prepared several hours before serving, just ensure that your gravy is piping hot, it will reheat the roast when poured on.

MSG: Instead of MSG, use a pinch of sugar in cooking, it brings out the natural flavour of foods.

SALADS: A pinch of sugar tossed in a salad enhances the flavour of each ingredient.

BAY LEAF: Place bay leaves in a bag or canister of flour. Keeps it weavle free.

DRY MUSTARD: Place a small piece of cardboard or kitchen paper inside the mustard container once opened. It stops it from getting hard and mildewy.

COCOA: Like mustard, place a piece of light cardboard or kitchen paper in the container once opened to stop it from getting hard.

FISH: Sprinkle fish with dried ground ginger, it takes the fresh smell and taste away.

FROZEN FISH: Soak in ½ cup evaporated milk for 20-30 minutes before use, it takes the freezer burn taste away.

METRIC COVERSION
How to convert measurements into equivalents of another system
Ounces to grams: multiply ounces by 28.3 to get grams
Grams to ounces: multiply grams by .0353 to get to ounces
Pounds to grams: multiply pounds by 453.59 to get pounds
Pounds to kilograms: multiply pound by 0.45 to get pounds
Ounces to milliliters: multiply ounces by 30 to get milleliters
Cups to liters: multiply cups by 0.24 to get litres
Fahrenheit to Celcius: subtract 32 from the Fahrenheit, multiply by 5, then divide by 9 to get celcius
Celcius to Fahrenheit: multiply celcius by 9, divide by 5 then add 32 to get Fahrenheit
Inches to centimeters: multiply inches by 2,54 to get centimeters
Centimeters to inches: multiply centimeters by .39 to get inches

OTHER MEASURES
3 teaspoons = 1 Tablespoon = ½ ounce
4 Tablespoons = 2 ounces = ¼ cup
8 ounces = 1 cup = ½ pound
16 ounces = 2 cups = 1 pound
32 ounces = 1 quart = 2 pounds
2 cups = 16 ounces = 1 pint
4 cups = 2 pints = 1 quart
1 quart liquid = 1 litre
16 cups = 4 quarts = 1 gallon

SUBSTITUTES

Nothing is better than the actual ingredient called for in a recipe but as we all know there are times when we start something and just simply do not have one basic ingredient to complete the dish. These substitutes are only here for emergency use not designed for standard substitutes.

CORN SYRUP: 1 cup sugar plus ¼ cup water boiled to syrup stage
        : equal amounts of honey
        : equal amounts of Golden Syrup

MILK: ½ evaporated milk plus ½ water
    : per cup, use ⅓ cup powdered milk to 1 scant cup water

HALF AND HALF: use same amount in evaporated milk

SOUR CREAM: per cup, use 1 cup evaporated milk plus 1 Tbsp. vinegar
    : use equal amounts of yogurt
    : per cup, use 1 cup cream plus 1 Tbsp. lime or lemon juice

CAKE FLOUR: Measure 1 cup of flour, remove 2 Tbsps. of the flour and replace it with 2 Tbsps. of cornflour. Sift before use.

SELF RAISING FLOUR: per cup, sift 1 cup flour with 1 ½ tsps. baking powder and ½ tsp. salt

CHOCOLATE SQUARES: Use 2 Tbsps. cocoa plus 1 Tbsp. butter per square or ounce required

CORNFLOUR: Use 2 Tbsps. flour per 1 Tbsp. cornflour required

FLOUR: Use ½ the amount called for in cornflour. For use in gravies, sauces etc.

SOUR MILK: Add 1 Tbsp. vinegar to 1 cup milk, let rest 10 minutes

BUTTERMILK: Add 1 Tbsp. vinegar plus pinch sugar to 1 cup of milk

DRY MUSTARD: Use 1 Tbsp. prepared mustard for each tsp. required

PREPARED MUSTARD: Use 1 tsp. dried mustard for each Tbsp. required

DRIED HERBS: Use ⅓ the amount required in fresh herbs

FRESH HERBS: Use 3 times the amount required in dried herbs

VINEGAR: For each Tbsp. required, use 1 Tbsp. fresh limejuice

CATSUP: Combine 1 cup tomato sauce with ½ cup sugar and 2 Tbsps. vinegar

TOMATO JUICE: Combine ½ cup tomato sauce plus ½ cup water

Misc - Hints, Tips, Substitutes, References

QUICK REFERENCES

1 Tbsp. Butter	= 1 oz .butter
1½ slices bread	= 1 cup soft breadcrumbs
1 slice bread	= ¼ cup fine dried breadcrumbs
4 ozs. dry macaroni	= 2¼ cups cooked
4 ozs. dry noodles	= 3 cups cooked
7 ozs. dry spaghetti	= 4 cups cooked
1 cup raw rice	= 2 cups cooked
Juice of 1 lemon	= 3 Tbsps.
Juice of 1 lime	= 1 Tbsp.
Juice of 1 orange	= about ⅓ cup
Grated peel of 1 lemon/lime	= 1 tsp.
Grated peel of 1 orange	= about 2 tsps.
1 medium onion	= about ½ cup chopped
1 cup whipping cream	= 2 cups whipped

Approximate guide for OVEN TEMPERATURES

	Celcius	Fahrenheit	Gas Mark
Very slow	120	250	1
Slow	150	300	2
Moderately slow	160	325	3
Moderate	180-190	350-375	4
Moderately hot	200-210	400-425	5
Hot	220-230	450-475	6
Very hot	240-250	500-525	7

REFERENCES RE THESE RECIPES

1 tsp.	= 1 Teaspoon
1 Tbsp.	= 1 Tablespoon
1 c	= 1 cup

Index

Index

Index

Index

Index

Index

Index

Index

Index

Index

My Recipes